KASHI

THE CITY ILLUSTRIOUS

OR

BENARES

KASHI
THE
CITY ILLUSTRIOUS
OR
BENARES

EDWIN GREAVES

GYAN

Published by

Gyan Publishing House
5, Ansari Road
Daryaganj, New Delhi-110002
Phone: 011-47034999, 9811692060
E-mail: books@gyanbooks.com

Distribution Network
gyanbooks.com
India, USA, Canada, UK, Australia, France

ISBN : 978-81-212-3663-8 (PB)
First Published, Allahabad, 1909

2nd Impression 2020

Printed at: Gyan Press, Delhi.

Kashi The City Illustrious or Benares
Author: Edwin Greaves

TO

ALL INTERESTED IN BENARES

AND

WHO SEEK HER GOOD

PREFACE.

Benares has not been unwritten. In 1868 the Rev. M. A. Sherring published his book, entitled "The Sacred City of the Hindus: an account of Benares in ancient and modern times." This is still the best book on the subject, though unfortunately it has been out of print for many years, and it is very difficult to procure even a second-hand copy. Quite recently, in 1905, Mr. F. B. Havell published "Benares the Sacred City. Sketches of Hindu life and religion." This is an exceedingly well written and enjoyable book; a vivid impression of Benares as seen by an artist and a thinker. The latest Government Gazetteer for Benares contains a great mass of information, but is somewhat packed away on shelves, not in show-cases. The Rev. Arthur Parker, who lived some years in Benares, wrote, in 1895, (republished in 1901) "A Hand-book of Benares," a most useful book, but now out of print, and not likely to be republished. Last year the Rev. C. Phillips Cape brought out a very readable and interesting series of sketches, entitled "Benares, the stronghold of Hinduism." The sketches include several subjects which do not peculiarly and exclusively relate to Benares, and some others which do, are not treated very fully.

PREFACE.

Thus there seemed room for such a book (call it "guide-book," "hand-book," "sketch") as this is intended to be. Many years' residence in Benares, and a very deep interest in all that concerns her, enables the writer not merely to repeat what others have written, but to add something as the outcome of personal enquiry and observation. In saying this he does not wish to ignore his very great obligation to those whose writings he has so freely used, but only to indicate that he has gone hunting, himself, and not *only* cooked the spoil of others.

Conscious of its many deficiencies, this little book is issued in the hope that it may prove of some service to visitors to Benares, and possibly to others who reside here for a season.

Whatever its fate, it is offered by one who is not only intensely interested in Kashi, but who loves her dearly, and desires, and strives for, her good.

EDWIN GREAVES.

BENARES :

June the 21st, 1901.

I must thank very heartily Messrs. Saeed Bros. of Benares, for the permission they have kindly granted me to have their photographs reproduced. Also I thank His Highness the Maharaja of Benares, very specially, for graciously placing at my disposal some very fine photographs from his collection.

E. G.

CONTENTS

Pronunciation of Indian Names and Words.

In the pronunciation of these :—

a	=	u	in	but.
á	=	a	,,	far.
e	=	a	,,	fate.
i	=	i	,,	fit.
í	=	ee	,,	feet.
o	=	o	,,	rope.
u	=	u	,,	full.
ú	=	oo	,,	fool.
ai	=	ai	,,	aisle.
au	=	ou	,,	south.

q, is a very deep guttural "k."

No attempt is made to distinguish the other consonants from the English consonants.

Panchganga Ghat and the Minarets.

CHAPTER I.

TRADITION AND HISTORY.

BENARES, or Káshí, "the illustrious," is a city of great antiquity, of unrivalled sanctity, and of boundless renown. So great is its antiquity, that its existence, apparently, long anticipates the dawn of history. It seems perfectly clear from tradition that Benares first existed, and then the rest of the world was formed round it. On equally good authority we find that the Benares thus referred to was not the Benares now included in the municipal limits, but the whole territory enclosed by the Pánchkosí Road. With facts like these before us who could dream of enquiring, "who founded Benares?" As well impertinently enquire, "who built the Himálayas?"

That Benares dates from very early times is a matter that admits of no doubt, and likewise that it was from very early times renowned for its religious associations. Some Puranic stories give a measure of plausibility to the theory that the Aryans made it one of their important centres, and that it has been, from time to time, a battle-ground for rival religions. There is a tradition that Mahádeva and his votaries were ousted for a time, and later on again resumed their sway.

It was clearly a place of no small importance five and twenty centuries ago, when Buddha made it the first centre for propagating his teaching, and it should be remembered that at that time Benares lay much nearer to Sárnáth than the modern city does.

It is in the 7th century of the Christian era that we first see Benares with anything like clearness, and, strange to say, the picture comes from China, it is the description given by the enthusiastic Chinese Buddhist traveller, Hiouen Thsang. He describes it as a city of about three miles long by one broad, thickly populated, materially rich, the people cultured, and paying honour to those who led a life of religious study. The pious traveller notices with great regret the fact that "few have respect for the Law," *i.e.*, for Buddhism, the greater part being believers in Hinduism. He refers to a hundred Hindu temples, and ten thousand heretics, (meaning, it must be presumed, Hindu devotees). This reference must be, however, to the *kingdom* of Benares, and not simply the city, for later on in his account, he speaks of "twenty temples of the gods," where apparently he is referring to the city.

If this be anything like an adequate account of the city at that period, the passion, or opportunities, for temple-building must greatly have increased since the days of Hiouen Thsang.

The names given to the city reflect little light upon its history, Baránasí and Káshí are both ancient names. Káshí is generally taken to signify "the shining," "the illustrious." Some people have accepted a dream-king Kásha as the founder of the city or kingdom, but this theory appears to have no historical foundation whatever. History does furnish references to the Káshís, as the inhabitants of the Kingdom of Káshí, but this throws no light at all on the question as to who founded the kingdom. The ancient form of the name Benares (more properly Banáras, pronounced something like the three English words bun-are-us) is Baránasí or Báránasí or Banárasí. To account for this last form a king Banár has been begotten of the imagination, but the only really historical references to any king Banár are to a monarch who must have lived long after the city had enjoyed the possession of this name. As an etymology for Baránasí it has been suggested that it was derived by combining the two words Barná and Assí, the two rivers which now form the northern and southern boundaries (roughly) of the city; but in the first place, the Assí ought not to be called a river, it is quite an insignificant stream, practically a dry watercourse for the greater part of the year, and in the second place, in ancient times the city appears to have been about the part where the Barná joins the Ganges, and only in more recent times to have spread out towards the Assí side.

Thus as regards the names for the city, we are reduced to the bald fact that many Hindus delight to speak of the city as Káshí, many others refer to it as Banáras, while Europeans spell and pronounce the name in a variety of ways.

The gentle Aurangzeb sought to purify the city from its idolatrous associations by renaming it Muhammadábád, but the name was never accepted and made current, it apparently only appeared in a few State documents. Probably few know that it was ever so named.

There are not wanting evidences, old ruins especially, to shew that the old city stood further north than it does at the present time, possibly on both sides of the river Barná, at the point where it joins the Ganges, it may even have been on the northern bank at first. Gradually it has been shifting south, and now stretches from about three quarters of a mile south of the Barná to the Assí, about four miles along the face of the Ganges, which at this part of its course flows, approximately, from the south-west to the north-east.

During the 11th and 12th centuries, or for parts of this period, it would seem that Benares was included in the kingdom of Kanouj, though to what extent it was subject to the central government it is impossible to say. There is mention in Mahommedan documents of raids of Mahommedans upon Benares during the 11th century, but nothing to justify the belief that Mahommedan supremacy was established.

At the close of the 12th century, however, an army from Shaháb-ud-dín Ghorí sacked Benares, and it is said, destroyed nearly a thousand temples, establishing a Mahommedan government, and leaving a governor in charge. Hinduism appears to have received a very severe shock, and it is recorded that many Brahmans forsook the sacred city and sought refuge in South India. Probably during the 13th, 14th, 15th, and 16th centuries Benares was more or less under Mahommedan domination, and Hinduism would have to "go softly," its measure of assertiveness being probably largely dependent on the character of the Governor for the time being, and the trend of matters in the adjacent dominions.

In the 16th century things greatly improved under the more liberal-minded policy of Akbar, and probably Benares during this period regained much of its former power as a centre for Hindu religious life. But during the troubled times that followed the death of Akbar the prosperity of Benares was no longer assured, and later on, the attentions of Aurangzeb marked a period of great trouble and humiliation for the Hindus of Benares. Aurangzeb swept down on the city in the year 1669, and left as a monument the mosque close to Gyán Bápí, which he caused to be erected on the ruins of the old Bishwanáth temple of the Hindus which he had destroyed. Probably it was at about the same time that another celebrated Hindu temple was demolished, and on its site the mosque erected whose lofty minarets from above Panch-gangá Ghát, form such a striking centre to the city, and seem to dominate the city from whatever direction it may be viewed, for miles round.

On the death of Aurangzeb there was another period of confusion and strife, and Benares had to pass through many vicissitudes. Eventually, in 1772, it was made over to Saádat Khán, the Nawáb Wazír of Oudh, who farmed it out to Mír Rustam Alí. It was at about this time that the foundations were laid for the enjoyment of the high position now held by H. H. the Maharaja of Benares. Mansá Rám, a Gautam Bhuihár, was the zamindar (squire) of Thithariyá, now called Gangápur, a village some nine miles west of Benares, and in which the ruins of a fort remain to the present day. Mansá Rám managed to extend his power, and in the end to attain the position which had belonged to Mír Rustam Alí. Eventually not only was this position confirmed to him, but upon his death the title of Rájá was granted to his son Balwant Singh.

Balwant Singh did not fail to improve the shining hour, and while keeping his master the Nawáb Wazír satisfied by the punctual payment of the revenue, he was steadily tightening his grasp of the province, until in 1748 he threw off all semblance of allegiance, and set up as an independent king.

Safdar Jang, the Nawáb Wazír of Oudh, was not likely to give up the province without a struggle, and summoned Balwant Singh to appear before him in Benares. This he declined to do and retired to the very strongly situated fort of Bijaigarh, lying away in the jungle, many miles to the south. Safdar Jang sacked the village of Gangápur, but eventually Balwant Singh was confirmed in his kingdom.

It was at about this time that he made Rámnagar his capital, and built a fort there. This remains the seat of the Mahárájá up to the present time.

During succeeding years Balwant Singh, between the various contending parties, had a distinctly lively time of it, but by dint of playing his cards well, and occasionally retiring to his jungle retreat, he managed to foil the efforts of Shuja-ud-daula, who had succeeded Safdar Jang as Nawáb Wazír of Oudh. Balwant Singh was befriended by the English and retained his possessions and power in the province, though he sometimes had to pay rather heavily for the maintenance of his position.

On the death of Balwant Singh in 1770 some difficulty was raised about the succession. The legitimate heir was Mahíp Nárâyan Singh, the grandson of Balwant Singh, by his only legitimate child, a daughter. There was a son, however, by a certain Rájput woman, and this son was old enough and clever enough to secure the succession for himself. He made large presents to the Nawáb, and thus strengthened his advocacy, and at a conference held in Benares in 1772, between the Nawáb and Warren Hastings, Chet Sing was confirmed in his kingdom, and in his title of Rájá. From the first, however, the relations between the English and Chet Singh were not particularly happy. At a time of severe pressure Warren Hastings demanded additional help from Chet Singh, which, while not absolutely refusing, he delayed and withheld. It was in August 1781 that matters reached a climax. Warren Hastings wearied by procrastinations and excuses, and stung by the attitude assumed by Chet Singh, sent the Resident with some sepoys to arrest Chet Singh, who was in his palace in Benares itself, at Shiválá

Ghát, on the bank of the Ganges. No resistance was made, Chet Singh was seized and left in the custody of two companies of sepoys, officered by three lieutenants. By a strange oversight, the sepoys had not been supplied with ammunition, and later on, some of the Rájá's soldiers from Rámnagar arrived. Under such circumstances what could be expected ? The forces of Warren Hastings were shut up in a narrow courtyard, comparatively unarmed ; they perished almost to a man, and Chet Singh escaped across the river to Rámnagar. The tombs of the three lieutenants may still be seen, close to the buildings at the back of Shiválá Ghát.

Lieut. Arch. Scott.
„ Jer. Symes.
„ J. Stalker.

killed August 17th 1781, near this spot, doing their duty.

An enclosure in the city close to the Chetganj Police Station commemorates the death of the Indian sepoys. This enclosure and tablet are far away from the scene of their death.

The position of Warren Hastings, with only some 450 men, was one of great danger, and he had to abandon the city and take refuge in Chunar. As soon as reinforcements arrived Warren Hastings returned to the city and re-established his position. Mahíp Náráyan Singh, the rightful heir to the throne, was now installed as Rájá, and the district was settled on a firmer and more permanent basis than had existed hitherto. The Rájá's possessions were now called "The Family Domains ;" in them the Rájá enjoyed defined jurisdiction, and still retained his title of "Rájá," but was no longer in a position to claim independent governing power.

The next event of importance occurred in 1799. Wazír Alí had succeeded to the position of Nawáb, but was deposed in favour of Saádat Ali Khán, the legitimate heir. Wazír Alí was granted a liberal pension, and resided in Benares, in the house and grounds known as Mádho Dás's Garden, the place where Warren Hastings was staying during the troubles just recorded. This garden is situated close to the Prince of Wales' Hospital, and is now occupied by the buildings belonging to the sect of the Rádháswámís. Mr. J. F. Cherry, the Resident in Benares, persuaded by the Collector, Mr. Davis, that the ex-Nawab was intriguing with disaffected Mahommedans in various parts of the country, decided to remove him to Calcutta. On January, the 14th, the ex-Nawab arrived with two hundred armed retainers to pay a State visit to the Resident. Mr. Cherry was seized from behind, and Wazír Alí attempted to stab him. He escaped into the garden but was pursued, and he, his Private Secretary (Mr. R. Evans), also Mr. R. Graham and Captain Conway were killed. Mr. Davis heard of the rising, and was soon threatened in his own house. He was living in what is called the Nadesar Kothí (now a State guest-house belonging to the Mahárájá of Benares, and situated close to the old Mint). Mr. Davis got his wife and two children on to the flat roof of the small tower of the building, and there joined them armed with a strong native spear. With this he managed to keep at bay, single-handed, his two hundred assailants. He stood at the top of the narrow winding staircase, and thus was in a favourable position to deal with his foes. News of the situation spread, and help arrived, and delivered Mr. Davis from his critical position. The Rájá of Benares, and the Delhi princes (then, as now, occupying the Shiválá Ghát buildings), remained loyal, and the ex-Wazír after a brief attempt to do further damage and then to defend his position in Mádho Dás's Garden, fled to Àzamgarh. Evidence was forthcoming to shew that plots had been formed, and had not prompt steps been taken, very serious difficulties might have arisen. As it was, Wazír Alí's rashness ruined the plots of the conspirators, and the incipient rebellion was soon at an end.

In 1809 a serious disturbance took place between the Hindus and Mahommedans. The mosque built on the site of the old Bishwanáth Temple had, ever since its erection, been a source of friction. An attempt on the part of the Hindus to erect a building between the mosque and the modern Bishwanáth Temple was resented by the Mahommedans, the quarrel came to blows, the Hindus mustered their forces and things were ripe for a widespread tumult throughout the city. The situation was one of peculiar difficulty, but Mr. Bird, the Collector, appears to have dealt with it promptly and tactfully. The city was not calmed down, however, without serious loss of life. The Mahommedans made an attempt to sack the Bishwanáth Temple itself, and later on the two forces of the contending parties met near Gáye Ghát, a congested part of the city with narrow lanes, and in the scrimmage many lives were lost. The next move was for the Mahommedans to attack Lát Bhairo, a sacred spot of the Hindus, situated on the Grand Trunk Road, not far from where the B. & N. W. Ry. crosses it, near to Ráj Ghát. The stone column, greatly venerated by the Hindus, was overthrown and broken, and has, since then, had to be encased in copper. The Hindus retaliated by desecrating and burning a mosque close by, and again many lives were lost. The next move was an attack by the Hindus on some mosques and tombs near to the Pishách Mochan Tank, at the opposite side of the city, and much destruction was effected. Troops were now forthcoming, but it needed much vigilance for a long time to prevent the feud again breaking out. It is said that during this time of turbulence not less than fifty mosques were destroyed, and several hundreds of lives lost.

A difficulty is said to have occurred in the year 1852 when some Nágars, resenting the judicial punishment of one of their number, raised a tumult, and induced the shop-keepers to close their shops, hoping in this way to rouse the people to discontent and disorder. Some loyal citizens came to the rescue, and getting supplies from the surrounding districts, broke down the success of the combination of Nágars and shop-keepers. The whole tumult was not, however, quelled without some energetic measures on the part of the Magistrate.

The Mutiny days brought their share of anxiety for Benares, but no disaster. As news was received from various quarters of rebellion having broken out, anxious consultations were held in Benares. It was well known that there were turbulent and disorderly elements in the city, and among the troops in Benares and Sultánpúr. Sultánpúr was at that time a military station, but has long been given up. It is situated a few miles south of Benares on a road to Chunar. There was only one company of European troops, the remaining troops were, a Sikh regiment, the 37th Native Infantry (Hindus recruited from these provinces), and a Mahommedan regiment (the 13th Irregular Cavalry). The latter regiment was called in from Sultánpúr, a careful watch was kept upon the city, and an attempt made to keep the populace good-tempered by endeavouring to keep the prices of provisions low. Some talk was made of evacuating Benares, but the policy was rejected. The Judge, Mr. Gubbins, seems to have been a tower of strength, the leading spirit both in deliberation and in action. It was decided that the Europeans should remain in their own bungalows, but in case of actual danger arising, they were to gather in the old Mint. It was further decided that an attempt must be made to hold the Collector's Court-house, as in the Treasury, which adjoins it, there were some very valuable jewels. English troops occasionally passed through Benares but could not be spared to remain here. It was on one such occasion that the opportunity was taken to disarm the 37th Native Infantry, which had been manifesting indications of restlessness. The attempt was made but it meant a wild and anxious time for a few hours, though the exact bearing of events does not come out very clearly. There were probably different elements in the different regiments, and it may be that the soldiers themselves did not understand very plainly what was being attempted, and how it would personally affect them. Under the circumstances we need not be surprised if the incidents were somewhat confused, both in their occurrence and in their record. Suffice it to say that there was some sharp fighting, and some splendid pluck and judgment manifested by a certain Captain Olpherts. Colonel Neill's coming was most opportune, and the dangerous days were passed during his stay of four or five days here. Some of the Indian servants of the Government also appear to have rendered valuable help, their loyalty, tact, and bravery being worthy of high praise. The state of the city caused considerable anxiety, for it seemed doubtful what might happen. The Rájá of Benares, however, remained loyal, probably many of the wavering ones took their cue from him, and threw in their lot with the loyalists. It was at that time that the old Rájghát Fort, lying between the present site of the Káshí Railway Station and the Barná River, was re-fortified, and from this position the city could be more easily overawed. These fortifications no longer exist, the ruins of them were probably broken down when the present Dufferin Bridge was being erected, but they must have remained standing for a long time. I recently travelled in a train, close to the spot, with an old soldier, who told me that he had been quartered in the Fort many years ago.

There were anxious and even difficult times in Benares until the Mutiny was quite over. Special powers were assumed by those in charge of the city, and martial law was proclaimed. Once and again threatened attempts by mutineers from without reached Benares, and on one occasion the Rajputs from Jaunpur marched to within nine miles of the city, but the attack was repelled.

At the time of the construction of the Water-works, when the demolition of a temple was being contemplated, there was a disturbance in the city, but this was of no political importance. It was apparently a little scrimmage stirred up by a few of the "badmáshes" (roughs) of the city, some of whom are ever ready for anything that may give a little zest to life, and yield an opportunity for a little looting. The temple was one of no importance, and still stands, islanded in by the Water-works and approached by a long walled way at the back of the Lalárak Kund.

It is a matter for much thankfulness that during the recent times of "unrest" affairs have been so quiet and happy in Benares. The city has had the advantage of possessing peculiarly able and sympathetic officials for many years, and the European and Indian residents enjoy times of mutual peace and contentment.

CHAPTER II.

BENARES IN 1909.

HAVING given a slight sketch of the past of Benares, let us now look at the Benares of to-day. In doing so it will be well not only to use our eyes, but to avail ourselves of such information as may come to us through the observation of others.

The city of the present time does not extend as far as the River Barná, but only to the point where the Dufferin Bridge crosses the Ganges. To the south it extends as far as the Assí. In the rainy season the Assí might, by courtesy, be called a river, but for the greater part of the year it is only a dry bed: in fact just where it joins the Ganges the bed is scarcely discernible, it is about level with the surrounding sand.

This long stretch of the city along the river front is between three and four miles in extent. It is crescent-shaped, and possibly there is not a city in the whole world which presents a more picturesque appearance than does Benares when viewed from the Ganges, or from the Dufferin Bridge. This river-front aspect of the city must have a chapter to itself.

The width of the city varies considerably. In the extreme south it is very narrow, but increases as it extends north. Taking a straight line from the Panch-Gangá Ghát in a north-westernly direction the city has a breadth of something like three miles, reaching as far as the old stone bridge over the Barná. To the west of this line at its northern end lies the European quarter, with the residences of many of the civilians and military officers, the barracks, and, beyond those, the railway quarters.

On the other side of the Barná are the principal Courts (the Commissioner's, the Collector's, and other Magistrates'), the Treasury, and a house occupied by the Lieutenant-Governor during official visits. Here also the Club has its home, with its Tennis Courts, Gardens, Swimming Bath, etc. At present the Judge's Court stands away from the others, to the south of the Barná, but materials are being collected for a new Court close to the Collector's. Near to the Courts are the residences of the Commissioner and the Judge, and some distance beyond those that of the Civil Surgeon. Opposite the Club is the Bank of Bengal, a modern well-built brick building, with its offices on the ground floor and the upper story used as the residence of the Manager. On a road running east from the Courts are the District Jail, the Cemetery, and the Kálí Shankar Asylum. This Asylum was endowed by the late Rájá Kálí Shankar Ghosal; it includes alms-houses for the blind, for lepers, and others, and has a dispensary and small hospital. The Civil Surgeon has the direct charge of the Institution, but its general management is under a committee. Along this road are several good residences. In former times these were official residences, but now many of them are occupied by private Indian gentlemen. To the north of this road are the Police lines and a large Lunatic Asylum.

The Provincial Jail is about a mile from the Club, on a road running west. This has extensive grounds, and is capable of accommodating 2000 prisoners.

For the European quarter to the south of the Barná, St. Mary's Church forms a good centre. Near to this are the two Hotels, Clarke's Hotel and the Hotel de Paris. West and north-west from these are various bungalows, the Military Hospital, the Assembly Rooms, the Masonic Lodge, the Military Cemetery, and due west the Hockey and Polo Grounds.

The Barracks lie between the part now mentioned and the Railway. They have quite recently been rebuilt.

On the main road leading from the stone bridge over the Barná (the bridge already mentioned) into the City, are several other buildings quite worthy of mention. To the left, lying back from the main road are the Judge's Court, and the London Mission High School. To the right are the Wesleyan Chapel, the Post Office, and the Medical Hall, this being both a druggist business and a printing press, though under different proprietors. Originally these were under one, the late Dr. Lazarus. Through this press Dr. E. J. Lazarus did a large amount of very useful work, Sanskrit, Hindi, and English, both for Christian and other literature.

Quite close to the Medical Hall is an old building called the Mint. This was the refuge for Europeans during the Mutiny scare. It belongs to the Mahárájá of Benares; for some time His Highness used it as a Guest-House, but more recently it has been occupied by the Kuár Sáhib, the son of the Mahárájá of Benares.

Opposite to this is the residence of the Wesleyan Missionaries. It may be appropriate to give here a list of the Mission premises of the various Missionary Societies in one paragraph, as they are very scattered. The London Mission has a Church and three Mission Houses near to the Cantonment Railway Station, (quite close to the adjacent level crossing). The Church Mission has its spacious quarters, consisting of Church, Orphanage, Girls' Normal School, and bungalows, at Sigra, about a mile on the road from the Railway Station to the Monkey Temple. The Church Mission has also a Church in the City, near to Dasáshwamedh Ghat. At Sigra also, very near to the premises of the Church Mission, is the Victoria Hospital, belonging to the Zenana Bible and Medical Mission. This Hospital has a branch dispensary in the very heart of the City also. The Zenana Bible and Medical Mission has another centre for work at Ramkatora, not far from the Queen's College. At Ramkatora also, on the Zenana Mission premises, is the Depôt of the Benares Bible and Religious Book Society, for the sale of Bibles, Christian books, stationery, etc. After this digression we must get back to the Medical Hall. Passing on towards the City, on the left is a fine house in extensive grounds called Nadesar House. This belongs to the Mahárájá of Benares, and is kept by him for the use of distinguished visitors. It was here that the Prince and Princess of Wales stayed when they visited Benares in 1906, and many other people of note have enjoyed the hospitality of the Mahárájá in this house.

Some distance further along this road, but standing well off the road, the Government College, Queen's College, is reached. Queen's College is an extremely fine building, possibly the finest of its kind in North India. No visitor to Benares should fail to drive round and see this College on his way to or from the City. It may lack the charm of the mossy lawns, the retirement, and the antiquity of the English Colleges, especially the Oxford colleges, but it has its gardens and its trees, and from certain points a good background of foliage may be obtained for the building, and it then strikes the observer as a building not only architecturally very fine, but of great beauty. In the College grounds are two houses, for the Principal and a Professor. Across the road is a High School (recently erected), and a Boarding House. In front of the High School is a very graceful column which is worth noticing.

The College grounds are being extended to the north-east, and on this ground is being erected a Library to contain the valuable collection of Sanskrit manuscripts, and books belonging to the College. In building, special provision is being made for the convenience of those who wish to visit Benares for special research work. As far as one can judge from the building in its unfinished state, stability and convenience are the ends mainly aimed at in the construction of the Library, there is no attempt to rival or even to equal the beauty of style displayed in the College itself.

After passing the Boarding House the main road bifurcates, one road running nearly due east to the Káshí Railway Station, the other south-east to Dasáshwamedh Ghát. This latter is the main carriage approach to the river, in fact the only one between Ráj Ghát at one end of the City, and Assí Ghát at the other.

Travelling along the first mentioned road, the Zenana Mission House and the Bible and Tract Depôt lie on the left. Further along on the right-hand side of the road are the Municipal Offices. Next on the left comes the Lady Dufferin Women's Hospital, and on the ground adjoining it the Prince of Wales' General Hospital. This latter was erected to commemorate the visit of our present King, when he came to Benares many years ago as the Prince of Wales. The Garden of Mádho Dás adjoins this, reference to which has been made in Chapter 1. A little distance beyond this is a fine large open space and some good buildings.

On the right is the Town Hall, presented to the City by a former Mahárájá of Vizianagram, who, although his dominions are so far from Benares, possesses some property here, and has made many generous gifts to the City. Benares owes very much to generous donors who are not its own citizens. Next to the Town Hall is the new and handsomely built chief Police Station, and beyond this the head Telegraph Office.

Opposite to these buildings are the Municipal Gardens. These are well kept up, and are a great boon to this very congested part of the city. At one corner of these Gardens, opposite to the Telegraph Office, is the Nágarí Pracháriní Sabhá Hall, a society devoted to the interests of Hindi literature.

This road needs little further description, it passes the Fruit and Vegetable Market, also the principal Grain Markets, then winds round an open space which was once the Machodárí Tank, but is at present in a very nondescript state. Possibly the Municipality may find the means at no distant date o finish filling up the Tank, and to convert this discreditable piece of waste ground into a public garden. Beyond this the road is comparatively void of interest and leads to the Káshí Railway Station.

We will now take the other road, already referred to as branching off by the Government Boarding House. This runs in a south-easternly direction and winds round at its end to Dasáshwamedh Ghát.

This is the finest road in the City, and has been opened out during comparatively recent years. Immediately on the left-hand corner is a large garden-house belonging to the Honourable Munshi Mádho Lál. Next to it is a walled enclosure sacred to the memory of the brave men who fell at Shiválá Ghát, as referred to in Chapter I. Next to this again is a Police Station, opposite to which are some fine buildings and grounds belonging to the Rájá of Hatwá, the representative of a very old Bengali family.

It may be noticed here that one of the features of Benares is the existence of properties belonging to noblemen who are not residents of Benares, yet regard it a desirable thing to have a building in the sacred city. In many cases these houses are seldom, if ever, visited by the owners, but are left in the charge of a few servants or retainers, or it may be, placed at the disposal of devotees, and may from time to time be lent as guest-houses for parties of pilgrims who journey to Káshí from that part of the country to which the owner belongs. It is a matter for regret that many of these buildings are not kept in better order, or sold to others who would make better use of them, and make them more worthy, in appearance, of the fine situations which they often occupy. Scattered over various parts of the city are really fine mansions, now fast becoming ruins, in fact, some of them are already so. The descendants of the original builders lack the interest, or the means to keep up the establishments, yet, apparently swayed by something of a dog-in-the-manger spirit, or perhaps entertaining a superstitious regard for possessing property in such a sacred city, will not let the property go out of their hands.

Passing along the road the Victoria Park is reached, more commonly known as Biniyá Park. This is an improvement of very recent times, and a very great improvement it is. It is easy to recall the (literally) howling wilderness of swamp and rubbish-heaps which it has replaced. At the end of this road as it bends round to Dasáshwamedh Ghát, is a church belonging to the Church Missionary Society, used principalty for evangelistic services for non-Christians.

Soon after passing this Church the road crosses, at right angles, another road, (which coming from the Chauk, runs parallel with the Ganges and reaches the extreme end of the City at Assí Ghát.) Crossing this, it shortly after bifurcates, and reaches Dasáshwamedh Ghát.

The road above mentioned may now be briefly described. This road starts from the Town Hall, and running nearly due south in a line with the Ganges, but separated from it by blocks of houses and temples, leads to Assí Ghát. At its right-hand corner, opposite the Town Hall, is a large group of buildings not yet finished; a temple and dharamshálá are being erected by one of the wealthy *raises* of the city in memory of his late father. A little further on is a new building belonging to the Wesleyan Missionary Society, used as a School and Reading Hall. A Hall belonging to the Arya Samáj rises by its side. Benares may be called conservative, and even benighted, by some of the up-to-date bustling moderns, but bigotry, taking the forms of bitterness and violence, are by no means rampant.

At the summit of a little rising ground stands the Chauk, an open space with a handsome Police Station on one side and shops on two others. Commercially this is the centre of the City. Branching away from this centre are narrow lanes with very high houses in which is hidden away much of the wealth of the city. One may wander for miles in and out of these intricate alleys. It is easy to lose oneself, for it is impossible to retain the sense of direction ; the alleys wind so much, and the houses are so lofty that the sun is seldom visible to the wandering passenger. Many of these houses are huge piles, with high walls, having only an insignificant doorway and tiny window-holes, reminding one not a little of some of the palaces in the Italian towns, such as Florence. Their real fronts must be at the back, if fronts they have. A ramble down these alleys will well repay the visitor the trouble. There are quaint doorways, and odds and ends of temples, even unexpected little scraps of gardens, there are trees in out of the way corners, giving shelter, at their bases, to sundry idols of quaint designs, (the trees themselves often being objects of worship) there are cows basking in sunless gullies, some of them occupying platforms which you wonder how they ever reached, there are blind alleys, and dust-heaps, and smells indescribable. And yet Benares is a healthy city. Let the visitor wander and wonder.

The Chauk presents a very busy scene in the evening. A very heterogeneous concourse of vendors of edibles and wearables and other commodities throng the south-east corner. Some of these have stalls, many have not. At other parts of the square, the carriages of wealthy merchants and others await their owners' exit from the narrow lanes in which their houses are situated, and down which no carriage can drive. Like many of the residents of the West End in London, these gentlemen have their stables and coach-houses in mews situated at some distance from their houses, there being this important difference that the Indian gentry cannot have their carriage driven up to their doors at the appointed hour, but must walk through the narrow lanes to the open street, or, if they be very careful of their dignity, be carried in palanquins. A miscellaneous assortment of loungers haunts the Chauk of an evening, some of them dandies of questionable social standing, many against whom the charge of dandyism could not justly be levelled. Altogether the Chauk presents a very striking picture of Indian life. This, however, is not so typical of Benares as many other scenes here found, for it is a scene which may be viewed in Allahabad or Lucknow, and some other towns in the United Provinces.

Passing on again from the Chauk southwards. On the left hand there is a refreshing little plot of garden and a fountain. Just beyond this, the Carmichael Library, with another scrap of garden and a fountain. There will be noticed also several large houses, of various styles of architecture and decoration. On the left hand, just before reaching the Dasáshwamedh Ghát Road there is a fine gateway leading to a temple enclosure. This gateway is quite modern, and is an exceedingly good specimen of modern stone carving at its best.

The continuation of this long road needs little in the way of description. It leads at first through the part of the City where many Bengalis have taken up their residence, and bears the name of Bengali Tola. There are some imposing-looking houses at various spots on the way. As Assí Ghát is neared, the Water-works are passed, or rather one part of them. This is the Pumping Station; the filtering and distributing is carried on at a second station called Bhadaini, situated some half a mile to the north-west.

Another main road which deserves some description is that which passing over the level crossing near the Cantonment Railway Station, skirts the City in a more or less southernly direction, and winding about, eventually terminates at the Ganges immediately opposite the Fort of Rámnagar, the seat of the Mahárájá of Benares.

The road is for the first half a mile, or nearly so, a part of the Grand Trunk Road. It passes the London Mission premises close to the level crossing. A little further along, on the left-hand side, there is a fine house and grounds, known as the "Parade Kothi," belonging to the Mahárájá of Vizianagram.

Nearly opposite the Railway Station the road breaks away from the Grand Trunk Road. At the bend a large Dharamshálá is being erected. Back from the road to the left, a little further along, but not visible from the

Stone Gateway near Gadaulia,

road, are a considerable number of Mahommedan buildings, mosques and tombs, these are mostly in a somewhat ruinous state. To the right of the road is a large open space walled round. This is a Namázgáh, (Mahommedan place of prayer). It is only used to any extent at one great festival during the year. The site was a present from the Mahárájá of Benares, himself a Hindu This affords another illustration of the breadth of view of modern Benares.

Some distance further along this road are the quarters of the Church Missionary Society, Girls' Normal School and Orphanage to the left, the Church, bungalows, and small Christian village to the right. The Victoria Hospital (Zenana, Bible and Medical Mission), is a few hundred yards along the road which turns sharp round to the left at Sigra.

Continuing along the road the Central Hindu College is reached, (on the right-hand side.) First comes the Boarding House, then the College. The best view of the College buildings is obtained from the other side. What was at first the front has now become the back, as the buildings have been greatly extended the other side and a good approach to them opened out from the main road after it ha taken a bend. On the opposite side of the main road stands another large group of buildings, connected with the Theosophical Society. These lie back from the road, and are only reached by a gateway, their proper entrance is by another road.

As the main road bends sharply round to the right there is a substantial building, which at first appears to be a part of the Hindu College, but has really no connection with it. It is a group of Alms-houses for the aged and friendless, built and endowed by the Rájá of Bhinga, who has for many years resided in Benares (beyond the Monkey Temple).

On the right, a little further along, is the filtering and distributing station belonging to the Water-works.

Separated only by a Jain Temple comes a palace belonging to the Mahárájá of Vizianagram. By the side of this is a Dispensary and small Hospital endowed by the Mahárájí.

A road continues straight on, joining the Assí Ghát Road, but the main road, leading to the Monkey Temple, and Rámnagar, turns sharply to the right by the Vizianagram Palace. Passing several large houses and temples, the finest being one built by the Ráni of Barhar, Durgá Kund and the Monkey Temple are reached. Immediately to the east of the Tank (Durgá Kund) is a garden containing the mausoleum of a Hindu Ascetic of some repute who died only a few years ago. Beyond the Monkey Temple the road is very pretty, and yields a delightful drive and splendid view of the city. It crosses the Pánchkosí Road and reaches the Ganges opposite to Rámnagar. In the morning the best view of Benares is perhaps from the Dufferin Bridge, but in the afternoon, when the sun is declining, this view from near Rámnagar is very fine. It takes in the crescent-shaped sweep of the Ganges, the flights of steps leading down to the river, the clusters of palaces and temples, and towering above all the minarets. It is a brilliant picture with the sun shining fully on it.

There are, of course, various other roads which are well worthy of description, but the principal have been given, and these must suffice. The visitor who has the leisure and the inclination will find enjoyment in seeking out others for himself.

Something must now be written about the residents of Benares, and their occupations.

The population at the last census (1901) was 209,331. Of these about 75 per cent. are Hindus, and the remaining

25 per cent. mostly Mahommedans. These numbers may surprise some people, who have been led to regard Benares as such an essentially Hindu city. As a matter of fact, the preponderating influence of the Hindus is not adequately represented by their numbers, they have a position and influence in the City far beyond their numerical strength. There is a small Christian community, also a few Jains, Sikhs, and just one or two Pársís and Buddhists (five only of each were recorded at the last census).

As regards the occupations of the people, industrial work employs a considerable number, the weaving of silk and cotton, and fancy embroidery works of various kinds. There is the fine silk weaving in which the patterns are produced by gold and silver thread woven with the silk. For these brocades or Kinkáb work Benares has a well-earned reputation. In addition to this there are other kinds of hand embroideries. Altogether these textile industries furnish occupation for something like 25,000 people.

Another industry affording employment for a considerable number is the Brass-work for which Benares is so widely known. It is said that there are over 600 factories, but such a word can only be used in a very loose sense, as both in this, and in other industries, most of the workers are not gathered into factories but do the work in their own homes. This system has several advantages, especially this, that it enables many women, widows and others to find occupation in the houses of their relatives, who would never dream of leaving the seclusion of their own homes to work in a factory.

A third industry which employs a few of the people is lacquered wood-work. The articles made are almost exclusively toys, and various small boxes, especially the "nests" of boxes, a large number of tiny boxes which fit one within the other. The lacquering is exceedingly well done. The articles are mostly in plain colours, or in bands, as the colour is fixed on while the article is still on the lathe. Practically all these toys are turned. At present, however, a rage is setting in for painting flowers, etc., on these toys, to the no small detriment of their artistic worth, for, as a rule, the flowers and other designs painted on them are but crude and tawdry work, and indicate the retrograde movement observable in so many indigenous industries, where the purely Indian type of work is being displaced in favour of feeble imitations of poor specimens of western inartistic productions.

Medical Halls and Printing Presses are popular institutions in Benares. There are over 50 Printing Presses, and the number of Medical Halls must be larger. To what extent these Presses and Medical Halls afford occupation and a livelihood to the proprietors is a question that may be left open. Two or three of the Printing Presses, however, are "going" concerns, and turn out a lot of work in English, Hindi, Sanskrit, and less in Urdu.

Possibly the occupation which affords a livelihood to a larger number of persons than any other industry is that of doing nothing. Many follow this avocation, and there are many patrons. We are not referring here principally to the professional beggars, of which there is no shortage. These do not live an entirely lazy life, but only secure their day's dole after vigorous appeals to the charitable, and, it may be, lengthy perigrinations. But quite apart from. this class, common to all great cities, though possibly here unusually strongly represented, there are well nigh countless Brahmans and devotees of various sorts and kinds who do nothing and live well. There are many well-endowed Chhattras or

Charity-funds, from which daily doles, in money or food, are distributed, largely to Brahmans, devotees, and widows. It has been calculated that through these charities provision is made for nearly 4,000 persons. There are many "maths" or monasteries, connected with the different sects of Hinduism. Many of these have large endowments, and afford shelter and provision for large numbers of the disciples of these sects. Quite apart from all these there are many Brahmans and "Sadhus" and "holy men" who are supported by the wealthy who accept the truth of the teaching, so profusely found in Hindu literature, that there is nothing more meritorious than gifts to Brahmans and devotees.

Among these recipients of bounty some are students, and the daily dole may be regarded as a scholarship. Others might, by courtesy, be spoken of as "private chaplains," but this does not involve peculiarly strenuous life.

The city is divided into eight wards: the Cantonments may be regarded as a ninth. From among these wards taking the northern part of the city first, are the Secrole, Jaitpura, and Adampura wards (taking them from west to east). Next come the Chetganj, Kotwali, and Chauk wards, the latter two reaching to the Ganges. Mainly south from these is the Dasáshwamedh ward, which stretches from the western boundary of the city to the river. South of this again is the Bhelupur ward which takes in the southern portion of the city and has a river frontage.

Benares is well off for communications with other parts of India. In former times there was a considerable river traffic, but this is now practically confined to the transit of merchandise, especially stone and wood. A ferry is maintained between Rámnagar and the outskirts of Benares, but most visitors from the other side of the river Ganges reach the city by train or cross the bridge by foot. Until recently there was a small toll for crossing the bridge, but this has now been abolished.

This Dufferin Bridge was completed in 1887. It is an iron-girder bridge, supported on very deeply-sunk stone and brick piers. It is between half and three-quarters of a mile in length, and cost a sum equivalent to more than £300,000. Vehicles are allowed to cross on the railroad itself, and for foot-passengers two side-ways are provided. It certainly affords a more easy if less picturesque entry into Benares than in the old days, when one had to walk or drive across the crazy and dusty bridge of boats, or, in the rainy season, take possibly an hour or so to cross the rushing flood in a boat.

Over the River Barná there are two good bridges, besides a railway bridge. There are also a ferry or two, and a road constructed over a dam, year by year, after the rainy season is over.

Benares is on the Grand Trunk Road. The part from the Ganges running parallel with the Oudh and Rohilkhand Railway, is now little used, until it reaches a point at the back of Queen's College. From that point, however, it is well kept in order, and passing near the Cantonment Railway station, goes west to Allahabad. A well-wooded road, with good camping grounds.

There are roads leading to Jaunpur, to Azamgarh, and to Ghazipur. Railway communications have been greatly improved during recent years. Twenty-five years ago there was only one line, the Oudh & Rohilkhand, from Lucknow into Benares by way of Fyzabad and Jaunpur. In 1887 the opening of the Dufferin Bridge enabled this line to connect with the East Indian at Moghal Serai. Later on, the Oudh & Rohilkhand opened a new line between Lucknow and Benares, by a shorter route, through Pertabgarh. Still more recently this part of the line has been connected with Allahabad by two different routes, and another bridge has been built over the Ganges, just outside Allahabad.

The Bengal and North-Western Railway has also been brought into Benares by a bridge built over the Barná. This connects Benares with the parts lying to the north and north-west, on the same side of the Ganges. This line has now been extended in the opposite direction towards Allahabad, in fact is open as far as Júsí, close to Allahabad. Another bridge over the Ganges is to be undertaken, which will take the line right into Allahabad.

The European population of Benares is not large, but is increasing, mainly owing to the larger staff on the Railways. There is the usual staff of Civilians, *plus* a Commissioner (as Benares is the centre of a Division, as well as of a district). There are the officers attached to a native regiment, and about two companies of European troops. European officers are in charge of the Divisional and District Jails, there are the members of the Railway staff, a fairly strong force of Missionaries, and a few others.

The city has been greatly improved during recent years. The Municipality, aided by the Government, has undertaken some big operations, such as the Waterworks, and a Drainage Scheme. Vast improvements have been effected in the matter of sanitation. A European idealist, visiting the city, upon hearing a remark of this character, discourteously expressed some curiosity to know what things were like before the improvements were effected, but he was evidently unfamiliar with the average condition of sanitation in the East, and we did not take him too seriously.

The Benares Municipality is a vigorous body of workers, and the condition of the City does great credit to their manifold activities. The Municipal Board consists of 29 members. Of these 15 are Hindus, 10 Mahommedans, and four others. The Collector is Chairman of the Board *ex officio*.

The supply of water, sanitation, the upkeep of City roads, part of the educational work, also the collection of income are some of their chief responsibilities. The chief sources of income are Octroi, Water Rate, House and other Taxes, and the rents of Municipal property. The Income last year was Rs. 565,000, and the Expenditure Rs. 600,000. In the expenditure were special items which are not expected to be recurrent. The deficiency was met by a balance in hand from the previous year. A Visitors' Tax is now imposed, which, it is anticipated, may yield an income of some Rs. 30,000. The financial position of the Municipality is, therefore, regarded as quite sound.

This sketch of the Benares of to-day is but fragmentary, and many items of real importance are left untouched, but it is hoped that it is tolerably accurate as far as it goes, and gives a bird's-eye view of the general condition of this interesting city. Benares is awake, and is moving with the times, if not quite as fast as some places. Possibly many of its "ancients" sigh over the times that are no more, and regard its religious glory as waning. Progress is being made, and it is believed that this is not only material but moral. Larger conceptions of life are being aroused and fostered, and the desire cherished of improving the environment and conditions of the life of the people as a whole.

CHAPTER III.

THE RIVER FRONT.

IN the present chapter we shall deal with that which is most characteristic of Benares, as far as the eye is concerned.

Architecturally Benares has not much to boast of, and must give precedence to many Hindu centres in different parts of India. Its temples are insignificant in size as compared with those in the south, though an endeavour is made to make up by number for that which they lack in bulk. The view of Benares from the river has, probably, no equal throughout the continent. From Assí Ghát to Ráj Ghát, a distance of three miles, there is a more or less continuous line of bathing-steps, surmounted by temples and other fine buildings. These things, however, do not complete the picture; the scene lacks its true effect without the busy throngs of people which stream down to holy Gangá Máí (Mother Ganges) in the morning. To pass along the banks in the evening is like walking through the *city* of London on a Sunday; it is without the bustling life, which is one of the most striking features of the whole scene.

This feature, of course, is not so important in a general view from a distance. In the morning the best view is from the Dufferin Bridge, in the evening from the road near Rámnagar at the other end of the City. The graceful curve of the Ganges here, approaching a crescent, gives additional charm to the picture. The wide stretch of water, the long flights of steps, the various groups of buildings, with the spires of the temples interspersed with foliage, a few quaint boats, and the minarets soaring heavenward above it all; these form a picture surpassingly striking.

In many respects the buildings cannot bear the slightest comparison with those of Venice, but even could the broad view obtainable of Benares be possible in the Italian city, it is quite open to doubt if the general view could be more strikingly beautiful. It is not the artistic excellence of the details, but the grouping of the whole, the extent, the very heterogeneousness of the buildings, the quaint irregularities, the ruinous patches, the temples and the trees; all these and many other features contribute to make the complete view one which stands quite alone, and possibly could not be surpassed in the whole world for genuine picturesqueness.

Quite another view is obtained from the top of one of the minarets. This not only gives a distinctly different view of the river line of the city, but a vivid conception of the city as a whole. One is able to realise, to some extent, what a congested population there is, and yet is surprised to find how that even in the most densely populated parts there are little patches of green (single trees or tiny gardens).

In attempting a detailed description of the river front, it might be thought that the best plan would be to start from Dasáshwamedh Ghát, work up the river and then return and work downwards towards Ráj Ghát, as this is the route so often taken by tourists. But there is no imperious necessity for viewing the Gháts in this order. We, therefore, take the Gháts as they come, steadily working, with the stream, from Assí to Ráj Ghát. Mention will not be confined to the Gháts themselves but to the buildings above them.

1. *Assí Ghát.*—Although this is the southern termination of the line of Gháts, it is not the most southernly point of the city. The Pánchkosí Road breaks away from the Ganges at Assí, and on it there are several temples and Akhárás, or Monasteries, and these should be included in the city. Just above Assí Ghát itself, slightly to the south, there is a temple of Jagannáth of some importance. In the large enclosure there are spacious court-yards, blocks of buildings and a temple. The whole place has rather a dilapidated look, and is not much frequented, except once in the year, when a Melá (religious gathering) is held at this spot. There are such innumerable temples in Benares, that it is difficult to keep them all going, and most of them have to be content to be publicly noticed once a year or so.

The Assí is a stream of some volume during the rains, but for the greater part of the year is a dry bed. The story runs that the goddess Durgá after achieving a victory, rested at Durgá Kund, at no great distance from this, and let fall her sword (assí means sword), and that this sword cut out in the ground, where it fell, the river Assí. There are points in the story which might suggest doubts to a sceptical mind, but a slavish attention to matters of topography and such trifles is beneath notice in traditions which have the hall-mark of antiquity.

The spot where the Assí meets the Ganges has great virtues as a bathing place. It is one of the "Pánch-tírath," or five specially sacred spots in the Ganges which should be successively bathed in. These five bathings should be performed on the same day to secure the esired merit. The five spots are:—1. Assí, 2. Dasáshwamedh, 3. Barná-sangam, then back to 4. Panchgangá, and 5. Manikarniká.

A confluence (sangam) of a stream with the Ganges is often regarded as a spot of special sanctity. There is the Barná-sangam, where the Barná joins the Ganges, the greatly reputed Sangam or Tirbeni at Allahabad, where the Jamna (and a third river not visible to the faithless) unites with the Ganges.

At the Assí end of the city the buildings lie back from the river, leaving a considerable stretch of sand. At Assí Ghát itself there are no stone steps for the bathers, but year by year after the rains have ceased, platforms of mud and sand are levelled up for their convenience.

Among the buildings above the river here there is a pretty little akhárá or monastery belonging to the Nának-panthís. With an inconsistency, by no means unusual, there is on the platform a small temple containing an image of Mahádeva. It is a remarkable fact that although several of the reformers, such as Nának, tried to eradicate idolatry, there seems to be a strong tendency for their followers to drift back into Hinduism, in which idolatry holds such a prominent position.

Next to this a new temple is being erected. This is a "Pánch-mandil," *i.e.*, five temples are grouped together. In one is Vishnu and Lakshmí, in a second Mahádeva, in a third Krishna and Rádhá, while in the fourth and fifth are duplicates of Rám, Sítá, and Lakshman, double honour thus being conferred on Rám, because he is the "isht-devatá" of the builder of the temple, *i. e.*, the specially chosen god, "the patron saint," so to speak.

A similar temple to this was built only a few years ago by another member of the same family. It is a very handsome building in a narrow road leading from the Monkey Temple to Assí Ghát.

Adjoining this is a new and somewhat dainty building recently erected by the Mahárání of Benares. This building is not regularly occupied, but is kept for use at special festivals.

2. *Lálá Misr Ghát.*—This is the first stone ghát, and is surmounted by a fine house. The well-finished, fluted stone columns at both ends of the building give it a very imposing appearance. The place has been acquired by the Rájá of Rewa, and is sometimes known by his name, but in India old names live long. New names may be given, but the old ones "hold their own." What has been, is, and will be for many a generation.

3. *Bájí Ráo Ghát.*—This is a continuation of No. 2 and also belongs to the Rájá of Rewa. Both gháts are commonly known by the one name of Lálá Misr Ghát.

4. *Tulsí Ghát.*—This again is two gháts rather than one but has the one name. The ghát and the building above it possess no beauty, but are of great interest by reason of their association with the name of Tulsí Dás. He lived in the corner building which surmounts the northern portion of the ghát. A sketch of his life is given in Chapter IX. The building is not a sightly structure. The occupants do not welcome visitors, but not to effect an entrance means no great loss. There are a few relics, but they are not of surpassing interest. There is a piece of wood on which the saint is said to have been wont to cross the Ganges, there are his sandals, and one or two others articles, which arouse the feeling that they may have been renewed from the bazaar once or twice since the dear old Gusáin passed away. The matter of relics of the poet is very unimportant, for he is enshrined in the hearts of the masses of the people by his "Rámáyan." Probably no religious poet of any age and country has

laid hold of his own and succeeding generations as Tulsí Dás has done. High and low not only revere his memory but can repeat many of his verses. Hinduism has never had a sweeter singer than Tulsí Dás.

5. *Water-works.*—Next in order comes the Pumping Station of the Water-works. Large pipes are carried out into the river, and these are arranged at different levels so as to tap the water at different heights, according to the season of the year. The water, having been pumped up, is forced along to the Bhelupur station, where it is filtered and distributed. There were many searchings of heart when the Water-works scheme was first mooted, and then constructed some 16 years ago. Could water, conveyed through pipes, be drunk by Hindus without injuring, if not absolutely ruining, their caste? But in the end difficulties were overcome: after all, Ganges water is Ganges water, even though conveyed through pipes, what can equal it? And now the water is greatly appreciated, and largely used (and wasted).

6. *Shrí Jánkí Ghát.*—This is a new ghát and is surmounted by a building containing several temples to Mahádeva.

7. *Bachráj Ghát.*—There are really three or four gháts which appear to be spoken of roughly under this one general name. Next to Jánkí Ghát is a strip of ground having no steps, above which is a Jain temple known by the name of Chhedi Lál. Then comes a flight of steps known as Rái Sáhib ká Ghát, the building above being in ruins. North of this comes a part called Imiliyá Ghát. (Imiliyá means Tamarind). Next to this is a building below which is a wall going sheer down into the river. In the building, on a slab of stone, is graved, "Prabhu Dás ká Ghát," but apparently Prabhu Dás never succeeded in popularising his name, and he never deserved to, seeing there is only a wall, instead of a flight of stone steps,

from which people could religiously bathe. Next to this is another stretch of river bank with no steps, and to this is also given the name "Bachráj Ghát." Close to this spot are some more Jain Temples.

8. *Shivála Ghát.*—This occupies a long stretch of bank, and is surmounted by an equally long row of buildings. These were the city-palace of Chet Singh, but were confiscated after the incidents referred to in Chapter I. The Ghåts are by no means popular with bathers, and the part has a deserted appearance in comparison with many other parts of the river-front. The buildings are considerably divided up, and some of the temples disused and in ruins. The houses to the south belong to the descendants of the Dehli princes. Apparently as the families have grown the place has been divided and sub-divided, and the general appearance of the whole place is not vividly suggestive of royalty. One of the members of the family is a well-known figure in Benares, and takes his share in the duties of the Municipality as a public-minded citizen.

The northern part of the building is divided between two sections of the Nágís, who profess to be followers of Shankara Achárya. There are numerous temples in their court-yards, most of them dedicated to Mahádeva, and having his images in them.

After Shiválá Ghát is an open space with no steps or buildings.

9. *Naipálí Ghát.*—This ghát boasts of no well-known name, but as it belongs to some member of one of the Naipálí families which are domiciled in Benares, it is sometimes spoken of as "Naipálí Ghát."

10. *Dandí Ghát.*—So called, apparently, from the fact that it was built especially for, or appropriated by, the Dandís, a class of ascetics, who carry about with them a long stick, the badge of their stage of the ascetic

life. Some holes have been bored in the stone steps, where they may fix up their sticks while they bathe.

At the top of this flight of steps is a small building connected with the name of Ballabhácharya. From it he is supposed to have either fallen or jumped—let us say, descended—into the river, and rising again in the form of a flame of fire, ascended to heaven.

11. *Hanumán Ghát.*—An interesting looking flight of steps, surmounted by a building possessing no pretensions whatever to architectural beauty, but substantially built and well kept. This is the third building belonging to the Nágás, a sect hailing originally from Rajputana. The ghát itself is refreshingly unlike the majority of those found along the river, being built of squarer blocks and arranged differently. "Anything for a change" is an excusable longing in Benares, where there is such a tendency to slavishly follow out not only one type of building, but to imitate in almost every detail. There is an ancient look about these steps, but there appears to be no reason to conclude that they have any advantage over many of the other gháts in this respect.

12. *Smashán Ghát.*—There is an open stretch of ground here reaching down to the river. This is a burning ghát, where bodies are cremated. No such sanctity attaches to it as pertains to the Manikarniká Ghát, but it is still used. One may conclude that in former days it was far more popular than it is now, as there are several stone memorials of "Satís" (suttees), which took place here, *i. e.*, widows being burned alive with their husbands' bodies. Of the eight memorial stones which are prominent, two are in a very superior style, being enclosed in shrines.

The ghát is associated with the name of Harischandra, one of the favourite heroes of benevolence, honour, and fidelity, held up for all good little boys to imitate. Harischandra was a king who treated his subjects with the utmost consideration. A famine of great severity visited his country, and the king expended all his great wealth in providing for his starving subjects. While still in the depths of poverty, a celebrated sage, the great Bishwámitra, came along, in great need of money. Harischandra did his best to satisfy his requirements, selling off everything he possessed, but still the needs of the saint were not met. Sooner than send away Bishwámitra with his wishes unfulfilled, Harischandra, as a last resort, sells himself, for a year, as a slave, to a "chandal" or "swapach," one of the very lowest castes, or rather outcastes, whose duty it was to attend to the burning ghát. This man supplies Harischandra with the needed money, and the king becomes his slave to do whatever degrading work may be given him. He is to keep guard at the ghát, and, among other duties, to exact the fees from the relatives of the dead. One day his own wife comes along, with the corpse of their only son. Alas! where is the fee to come from? In vain Harischandra demands it, pleading that faithfulness to his master necessitates his exaction of the fee. The wife pleads that her single garment is the only article she possesses in the world. There is no help for it, that must be given. She has already seized it to tear it off and pay it as the cremation fee, when the three worlds quake, God descends from heaven, and appears to his faithful ones, the son is restored to life, chariots come down from heaven and bear the three away. It was at the ghát we are writing about that this incident occurred.

Near the burning ghát is a high platform built up, at the top of which there is an image of Mahádeva. Not far away is a small shanty occupied by an "Aghorí." The Aghorís are a special sect, who are worshippers of Mahádeva, and are supposed to be so released from any possibility of earthly defilement that nothing is unclean to them, they may eat anything, even corpses. Possibly some keep up the worst traditions of the sect, but it may be hoped that in most cases the liberty allowed in matters of food is not exercised to the full.

13. *Láli Ghát*—A long narrow flight of steps.

14. Next to this is a building belonging to some distant Rájá. It is interesting as illustrating what a monstrosity of ugliness may be accomplished with bricks and mortar, when only properly arranged. The building has no flight of steps.

15. *Ijánagar Ghát.*—This has been recently built by the Rájá of Ijánagar or Vizianagram. A neat little ghát surmounted by an equally neat and well-finished house.

16. *Kedár Ghát.*—The most popular ghát at this end of the City. It is greatly resorted to by Bengalis. At the top of the lower flight of steps is a small reservoir called Gaurí Kund. The water of this also has its special virtues, and may supplement any deficiencies not obtainable through a bath in the Ganges. Gaurí is another name for Párvatí, the consort of Shiva.

The temple at the top of the second flight of steps is of no great size or beauty, but is striking by reason of its unusual colouring, being painted in red and white stripes (perpendicular). The temple is Kedáreswar or Kedárnáth, *i.e.*, the lord of Kedár, Kedár being a place on the Himálayas where Mahádeva is said to have resided at one time. Within the enclosure is a central temple surrounded by smaller shrines.

17. *Chaukí Ghát.*—Recognisable by a pipal tree which can be seen at the top of the steps. The lower part of the tree has been built round with masonry, and on this platform are sundry deities, especially snakes.

18. A stretch of some distance with no stone steps. Above this is a building of some size belonging

to a certain Kumár Swámi, who owns other property near.

19. *Someshwar Ghát.*—So called by reason of a temple to Someshwar at the top of the ghát. Soma means the moon, and to her are attributed wonderful powers of healing.

20. *Mánsarowar Ghát.*—The name survives, the ghát has disappeared, that is, the stone ghát, except a small part of the upper part of the steps. The name comes from the Mánsarowar Tank, which is situated not far away.

21. *Nárad Ghát.*—So named from a temple to Náradeshwar which surmounts the ghát. Nárad was a famous rishi or saintly teacher. In the West, the man does well who gets sainted after his death. In India it is possible to be sainted while living, and deified after death. There are several temples in Benares erected to the glory of rishis, such as Kapil, Vyás, Shankarácharya and others. Bháskaránand, whose mausoleum is near the Monkey temple, was both sainted and deified during his lifetime, and had a temple with his image in it in the garden in which he lived.

22. *Rájá Ghát or Amrit Ráo Ghát or Rájá Bináyak ká Ghát.*—Above this is a very massive building, with small projections in stone studded all over it. This is a well-endowed religious house providing for the support of a hundred Brahmans.

23. *Dhobi Ghát.*—This name might be enjoyed by this and several other spots on the river bank. The dhobies (washermen) take possession of several of these places where there are no stone steps and carry on their work. One might have expected objections to the Ganges being used for such a very commonplace purpose, within the bounds of the Sacred City, but apparently none are raised. The Hindus believe so strongly in

6

the virtue of Ganges water that they probably conceive it impossible that anything could defile it. They appear to have no scruples against bathing in Ganges water close to where a sewer runs into it.

24. *Annapúrná Ghát.*—Also sometimes called Gangá Mahal ká Ghát.

25. *Pánde Ghát.*—Indicated by a banyan tree at the top, under which are many images of Mahádeva. Not far from the tree, lower down, is a red temple which also contains an image of Mahádeva.

26. A stretch with no stone gháts surmounted by a large pile of buildings belonging to the Rájá of Nattor.

27. *Chausathi Ghát.*—A flight of quite unconventional steps. Quite a relief to those who have not to climb up them. To the north of these steps is a somewhat unconventional pile of buildings, the abode of holy men.

28. *Ráná Mahal Ghát.*—Belonging to the royal family of Udaipur, one of the Rajputana States. Most of the steps are in a very dilapidated condition, but one long flight from the doorway right down to the water is quite sound. Above the gháts there is a long rambling block of buildings, with a rather woe-begone look about them.

29. *Munshí Ghát.*—Built by Munshí Shrí Dhar. The southern portion now belongs to the Rájá of Darbhanga. This ghát and the massive building above it rightly rank as one of the most imposing pieces of architecture along the river front. The central fluted columns and the octagonal ones at the end are bold and striking.

To secure beauty in the structures on this river front is a matter of great difficulty. A rise in the river of 40 feet or so has to be allowed for, consequently a large part of the lower portion of the building must be quite solid. This imposes severe limitations and grace is hardly to be expected under such circumstances.

Sitla Ghat.

30. *Ahalyá Bái Ghát.*—This fine ghát and the building which surmounts it (and also several other buildings in Benares), perpetuate the memory of a very remarkable woman. Her son, while quite a lad, became the ruler of Indore, but died insane soon after his accession. Ahalyá Bái assumed the reins of government, and ably seconded by the Commander-in-Chief, Tukají Ráo, successfully administered the affairs of the State for 30 years.

31. *Sítlá Ghát.*—This is crowned by a small whitewashed temple, in which Sítlá Mái (Mother Small-pox) is worshipped. The idea is not so much to avert smallpox altogether as to secure the favour of the goddess and thus escape lightly.

32. *Dasáshwamedh Ghát.*—This is practically the central ghát in the city, and the only one which has a carriage approach to it there. It is not only central in position, but is a spot of great sanctity. The name means " the ghát of the ten-horse sacrifice." Of course, there is a legend about this name, and it is of interest on account of its connection with the name of Divodás. This mysterious Divodás is credited with having turned all the gods out of Benares, including Shiva. It has been conjectured that this Divodás may have some connection with Buddhism, and that the story of his having turned the gods out of Benares may be connected with the growth of Buddhism by which idolatry received, for a time, such a severe check. The story runs that Shiva and his consort Gaurí were discussing the position of affairs between themselves as they abode together at Mandráchal. They decided to obtain the help of Brahmá, who should go to Benares and see if he could not in some way or other mend matters. Accordingly Brahmá mounts his steed, a goose, and is away to Benares. He cogitates how he can overthrow Divodás

by involving him in some sinful act which will weaken his power, and thus open the way for the return of the ejected gods to Benares. The plan he adopted was to ask from Divodás the necessary materials for a special sacrifice, knowing that if any mistake were made in any detail Divodás would incur sin and thus be undone. Brahmá makes his request and takes his seat at Dasáshwamedh Ghát. The necessary materials for, not one but ten, sacrifices are duly sent, and are exactly right in every particular. Brahmá then offers up the ten-horse sacrifice. The ghát is thus consecrated for ever, and henceforth to bathe here is as efficacious as bathing at the Tribeni in Allahabad. Brahmá, unsuccessful in his original mission, is ashamed to return to Mahádeva, and settles down contentedly in Benares.

The details of this story do not favour the theory of Divodás having been a Buddhist King, otherwise he would hardly have agreed to supply the materials for sacrifices.

At this ghát are two images, Dasáshwamedheshwar and Brahmeshwar, the worship of which is supposed to secure deliverance from the necessity of future births.

Immediately above the ghát, on an elevated platform, is a prominent temple, but it seems to be of very little importance in the eyes of the people, being little visited. Many of the fine temples are of small account, some of the most celebrated are very unattractive to the ordinary observer.

This ghát has a commercial as well as a religious importance. At its northern end there is a landing-place for merchandise, and large quatities of stone and other materials are landed here. The huge quantities of stone often found stacked on the bank above give some indication of the prosperity of the City, in which new and imposing buildings are continually being erected.

Dasashwamedh Ghat.

33. *Mán Mandir Ghát.*—This belongs to the observatory which stands above it. This observatory, together with four others of a similar character, at Delhi, Ujain, Matará, and Jeypur, were built a little more than two centuries ago by Rájá Jai Singh of Jaipur, who appears to have had a passion for astronomy, and attained a wide reputation for his attainments. Whether he named the observatory after his distinguished ancestor Mán Singh, in honour of his memory, or whether he utilised a building or site which already bore that ancestor's name is not clear.

The place inside is not much better than a ruin, but a very well-preserved ruin. The astronomical instruments were massively constructed of stone and metal, and are still is very good preservation, though unused. The place is no longer used as an observatory, but is occupied by a few men, presumably pensioners of the Mahárájáh of Jaipur. They do not suggest to the casual visitor that they are guilty of much astronomy.

The building of Mán Mandir is a large, and, in a sense, an impressive pile, but it is too flat to be called beautiful. It lacks grace and symmetry. There is one redeeming feature, however, and that is very redemptive. High up in the extreme north-east corner of the building juts out a balcony, which is one of the finest things in Benares. It is a gem, and well worth examining carefully. It is seen well from the river, but better still from the ghát itself standing in a north-easternly direction from it. It has been conjectured that this may have come from some older building and been built into the present one, and this conjecture seems plausible.

At the south of the building. approached only by a flight of steps, (unless you can prevail on one of the attendants to let you through by a door from the observatory part of the building), is an " akhárá " (which means here gymnasium). On the platform outside athletes may frequently be going through their exercises. There are many such akhárás in Benares. The various exercises, differing so widely from those common in the West, are distinctly interesting. In India, gymnastics are carried to great proficiency. The "training" so far as concerns diet, must be very distinct from that adopted in the West, the athletes are, generally, not wiry, but great masses of flesh. The first impression might be that it is all flesh, not muscle, but after seeing their feats of strength and agility the conclusion would be reached that such an impression was a mistaken one.

34. *Tripur Bhairaví Ghát.*—So called from a temple to Tripur Bhairaví in a lane above the ghát. This temple is noticeable for two large carved-stone human faces, one on either side of the doorway, close to the ground. There are several other temples between the top of the ghát and the temple of Tripur Bhairaví.

35. *Mír Ghát.*—A narrow but well-built ghát, leading up to a number of temples. Close to the top of the steps is a monastery belonging to the Nának-panthís (Sikhs). The sect is somewhat strongly represented in Benares. The members of the sect dwelling at Mír Ghát, belong to the "Udási" section.

36. *Napalese Temple.*—Below the temple there is a strongly built wall by the river, and in it are some ladder-like steps leading down to the water. There is no ghát in the usual sense of that word. The temple, half hidden among the trees, with its (for Benares) uncommon architecture, and its gilded bell-shaped pinnacle, is very picturesque. The temple, together with a guest-house attached to it, is not built of stone, but of brick-work and wood, the latter of which is very elaborately carved. The carving of the guest-house is exceedingly good,

that of the temple is ruined by the gross indecency of some of the details.

37. *Lalitá Ghát.*—A small ghát, the upper part leads through a gateway into the city. Outside this gateway, or rather small building, may be noticed on the wall what at first look like a pattern, painted in red on a white background. This, on examination, proves to be the name of "Rám" repeatedly painted. To repeat the name of Rám either by writing, or by the voice, is a most efficacious act of worship. Handkerchiefs are thus printed with the name of Rám all over them. I met a man once, whose practice it was to daily write the name of Rám a thousand times on leaves of a tree, and then destroy them.

38. *Ráj Siddheshwarí Ghát.*—This adjoins Lalitá Ghát. From the gateway, referred to above, a passage leads into a long pile of buildings bearing the name of Ráj Siddheshwarí. The buildings wear a forlorn and desolated appearance, and apparently give shelter to only two or three members of a sect said to have been founded by a certain Siddh Bábá. Possibly some wealthy patron of the founder of the sect provided them with this commodious home, but the sect has not grown, and thus the " empty house."

39. *Jalsaí Ghát.*—There is now a series of three ghâts, which apparently bear the common name of Jalsaí. It is singular that this ghát, which is *the* cremation ghát for the City, should be connected, by name, with Vishnu, when Benares is so very largely devoted to the worship of Shiva (Mahádeva) rather than Vishnu. Jalsaí is one of the names of Vishnu, meaning " the sleeper on the water." Is it just possible that the name is not here applied to Vishnu, but to the dead? That as we speak of the dead as " sleeping in the grave-yard," so the Hindus speak of theirs as sleeping in the Ganges? One would like to read such an idea into the name.

The ghát to the south might be called Umráogír Ghát as the building immediately above the ghát bears his name.

Above the second ghát is an old temple (Shiválá) connected with the name of a certain Rájá Rám Bal-lam. Like a similarly constructed and situated Shiválá at Dasáshwamedh Ghát, this appears to have failed to obtain popular favour, and is neglected and little used.

At present the ghát below is used as the burning-ghát, but this is only a temporary arrangement while the proper burning-ghát is being re-built. One might say "built" not "re-built," for at first there was little in the way of masonry. There was the shelving bank of the river levelled in places for the pyres to be built up and consumed. Recently some of the citizens felt that this unsatisfactory state of things ought not to be allowed to continue and decided to build a burning-ghát worthy of such a city as Benares. Considering the many thousands of people who come to Benares to die, it seems but fitting that some better arrangements should be made for their cremation. From statistics of Births and Deaths in Benares one might be led to conclude that Benares is a peculiarly unhealthy city. For the last two years the figures are, 1907-08 :—Births 9,680. Deaths 10,679. For 1908-09 :—Births 8,471. Deaths 10,686. The real explanation of the figures is that so many people come to Benares in their old age to die, and that there are so many Sádhus, who are celibates.

The new burning-ghát which is being erected promises to be a very substantial and handsome structure. Babu Moti Chand has been the leader, I understand, in the movement to get this ghát built, and has been a most generous donor towards the heavy expenses involved in carrying it out.

BURNING GHAT—MANIKARNIKA.

Raja of Amethi's Temple.

The next ghát is singular in having screen work at the back of it between the bathing steps and the footway which runs along above them. Part of this ghát appears to be reserved for the use of women.

From this spot a lane leads off to the Golden Temple. It is an exceedingly interesting lane, it is crowded with temples, many of them being very finely carved.

40. *Manikarniká Ghát.*—To Hindu pilgrims this is perhaps the most sacred spot in the whole city, it certainly is the most crowded at the great festivals, and to the European visitor will prove the most interesting. There is not a more picturesque scene anywhere in Benares than is presented here at the time of a big "nahan" (bathing festival). Looked at from the river, there is in the centre the dense crowds of people on the footway by Manikarniká Kund; as a background to these, a strange medley of temples and buildings with the red-domed temple of the Rájá of Amethi towering above them all; in the foreground a leaning temple and porch, almost on a level with the water, and threatening to topple over into it, and the eager crowds of bathers from various parts, in their various styles of dress, and exhibiting a variety of colouring. It is a sight that will be long remembered by the visitor.

The temple close by the river has evidently been undermined by the water and is much out of the level. The upper part of the porch is defective. Formerly this was the temple of Tárakeshwar, but apparently some fears were entertained about the safety of the god in this shaky building, accordingly another temple was built for his accommodation, about 117 years ago, and the god transferred to it. This temple is higher up the bank and further to the south.

Manikarniká Kund itself is not a peculiarly attractive spot, and it must for ever remain a wonder to the foreigner how people can accept the traditions, and seek to cleanse their souls from sin by venturing down the steep stone steps, and plunging into the very uninviting big puddle of water at the bottom. The whole place is under water when the river is in flood in the Rainy Season, and the tank becomes partly filled with mud and silt. After the rains are over, the tank or kund has to be cleaned out, but East is East, the work proceeds but leisurely, and meanwhile the bathers have but a poor time of it. At a festival one may see the eager souls swarming down into what is simply mud, it may be that in one corner a hole is dug where the mud is rather more fluid, but only the favoured few can get near this coveted corner. Fortunately it appears to be the custom to bathe in the Ganges after taking the dip in the Manikarniká Kund, and this somewhat relieves the situation.

Manikarniká means "ear-ornament," and various traditions are current to explain how the Kund came to bear this name. One is that one day while Vishnu was seated by the pool, Mahádeva came along, and seeing the glories of Vishnu reflected in the water could not restrain his admiration but burst out into raptures of praise, and offered to grant Vishnu any boon he cared to ask. Vishnu asked that Mahádeva would abide with him. This compliment so thrilled Mahádeva with emotion that as he quivered with delight his ear-ornament dropped into the pool. Who can wonder that with such stories as this clustering round it, the pool should be supposed to possess great virtues.

Near to this spot is a marble slab carved with two raised foot-prints, this is styled "Vishnu páduká," and marks one of the spots where Vishnu walked. This also calls forth the reverence of the devout Hindu.

On the stone platform on which these footprints appear, occasionally a cremation takes place instead of at the usual burning-ghát, but this honour is reserved for very distinguished people indeed.

41. *Dattátreya Ghát.*—Just above this ghát is a small temple which has a touch of individuality about it, if not much in the way of beauty. Inside is a "pádu-ká," the footprints of the great Brahman saint and teacher Dáttatreya, in whom, parts of all the three deities, Brahmá, Vishnu, and Shiva, are said to have become incarnated. The temple is on a level with the footway above the ghát. Every rainy season when the river rises, it works away behind this temple, making deep fissures, and threatens to carry it away. The river appears to be peculiarly dangerous to the land at this point, possibly there is some back current. This may account for the wreck of the Scindiá Ghát now to be noticed.

42. *Scindiá Ghát.*—It was evidently intended to build a ghát and mansion here which should eclipse all the others along the river, but like many another ambition it was never realized. The ghát remains, though by no means in a perfect condition. The building which was to have crowned it has come hopelessly to grief. There are stories about underground rivers (such imaginary rivers appear to be rather popular). It is, of course, possible that there may be underground an old nala or drain, but probably the foundations were not deep enough, and were undermined by the river. The massive but fallen walls remain as a monument of a magnificent "might have been."

43. *Sankathá Ghát.*—Above the ghát is a temple with an image of Sankathá Deví, and a hostel for pilgrims and students.

44. *Gangá Mahal* or *Gwáliar Ghát.*—The building above this ghát is one of the finest along the river front. It belongs to Gwáliar, a very important Native State

in Central India. There are octagonal columns at each end, and a very massive round pillar in the centre. The three are surmounted by graceful balconies, and a three-storied building lies at the back of these. Somewhat curious are the two flights of steps, which starting from the sides of the central column ascend to the tops of the outer ones.

45. *Ghoslá Ghát.*—This is surmounted by a building which is a worthy companion to the one mentioned above. It was founded by one of the great Maráthá houses, the Ghonsla or Bhonsla family of Nágpur. At the ends of building are massive fluted columns. Above, a gallery with stone pillars runs the whole length of the building. The flat front is somewhat relieved by a doorway in the centre, which leads up by a flight of steps to a temple within. This temple is somewhat peculiar in being painted, this gives it a very gay appearance.

46. *Ganesh Ghát.*—An unimportant ghát. Next to this is what might appropriately be called "*Wood Ghát,*" for vast quantities of wood are landed and stacked here, and sold for consumption in the city. The buildings above are in a peculiarly ruined condition.

47. *Rám Ghát.*—This is surmounted by an ochre-coloured building, in which is a quaint collection of idols associated with the worship of Vishnu, in his incarnation as Rám.

48. *Jaráo Mandir Ghát.*—This distinctive name may not be very common, but is given on account of the building which surmounts it.

49. *Bájí Ráo or Lakshman Bálá Ghát.*—Above this is a large but very plain structure, built by Bájí Ráo, one of the Maráthá Peshwás. The long and lofty front of this pile of buildings is but partially relieved by a great number of small windows. This house adjoins the great Mosque of Aurangzeb.

Ganga Mahal Ghat.

50. *Chor Ghát.*—This is said to have gained its name from the fact that the narrow flight of steps, which leads between the labyrinth of buildings above, offers peculiar facilities for a thief to escape, after robbing any of the bathers at the gháts below. "Chor," however, not only means *thief*, but has an idiomatic use which might suggest that the name was given because here bathers might slip down almost unobserved and take their baths.

51. *Panch Gangá Ghát.*
52. *Beni Mádho Ghát.*
53. *Durgá Ghát.*
54. *Brahmá Ghát.*

These are taken together as they form one continuous line of gháts, and it is not easy to decide where one leaves off and the next one begins. As a matter of fact it is not uncommon for the whole group to pass by the name of Panch Gangá Ghát. This name which signifies "the five Ganges" or "the five rivers," indicates that four other rivers here meet the Ganges. These do not meet the vision of the ordinary observer, and have dealt more kindly with the huge flights of steps and intricate masses of masonry above, than the imaginary river, which played havoc with the Scindiá Ghát. From an architectural standpoint this spot far surpasses the Manikarniká group of steps and buildings. It is well to have the boat taken out a short distance so that the visitor may take in at one sweep the picture presented. In the foreground the busy scene by the water's edge, the many bathers with their various-coloured garments, the little shrines dotted here and there among these lower steps, the streams of people on the footway, then above this, the long flights of steps running in different directions to the city above, the archway at the head of one particularly steep flight of steps, the quaint buildings tumbled together in indescribable confusion, and crowning the whole, the Mosque and Minarets of Aurangzeb. It is certainly a wonderful picture, and may well fascinate all who have the slightest appreciation of the artistic and the picturesque.

The mosque was built on the site of a temple demolished by the devout and gentle Aurangzeb. What a cruel irony to have put it here right in the very heart of Hindu sacred shrines, and the irony is increased by the fact that the mosque is generally known by the name of a Hindu, namely "Mádho Dás ká Daurhá." Mádho Dás is a purely Hindu name, borne apparently by the architect who carried out the wishes of the Mahommedan Emperor.

Below the mosque, but high above the river is a peculiar stone cone, a "Díwat," or lamp-stand, on the numerous spikes of which little lamps are fixed at a special Hindu festival.

Quite close to this is a small covered platform, containing another "Pádukà," the footprints of Rámánand, who may be called the father of many of the great Hindu Reformers. A slight sketch of his life is given in Chapter IX.

Some quaint temples are to be found near to the steps leading into the mosque enclosure. In one of them a female devotee tends the idol, this is very unusual. On a piece of open ground near by, a member of the Sádhu tribe makes his quarters. At times he may be found reading his religious books gracefully reclining on his bed of spikes. He may not represent Hinduism at its worst, neither is he a specimen of its best. His vigils and austerities do not appear to have greatly told upon his health. It is to be feared that his poverty stands in the way of his having his spikes properly attended to, they sadly need sharpening up. A woman Sádhu dwells at the same place, and occasionally affects the spiked bed, when it is disengaged, which it often is.

It's a tough climb up to the top of the minaret, but for any one under 16 stone, and not asthmatic, it's worth the trouble. From the river there are many steps to be ascended before the level of the mosque is reached and to get to the top of one of the minarets means another 140 feet or so. Reaching it, you have the whole of Benares at your feet. The way that the buildings are packed together is a marvel to behold, not rows of houses as there would be in England, but houses and temples of all sorts and sizes thrown together with a delightful scorn of anything approaching to order. I know of houses being so built that they can only be reached by passing through another. This other having to leave a covered passage right through it, reminding one of the covered way, to the stables, through the building, in some old-fashioned inns in England.

Several Jain temples lie close to the mosque. On a clear day Sárnáth can be seen in the distance. It will be noticed that in spite of the way that houses are crammed together, gardens and trees peep out in wondrous fashion. Trees sometimes appear coming right through the roof of a house.

55. *Ráj Mandil Ghát or Sílli Ghát.*—The ghát itself is a small one, but beyond it is a long line of somewhat dilapidated buildings bearing the name of the Rájá of Kotáh Bundí. These buildings are on the top of a high embankment wall, the base of which is close to the stream of the Ganges even in the hot weather, and is washed by it in the rains. It may be noted that then the Ganges may rise some 40 feet or more, and the footway which runs between the bathing gháts and the buildings above them is submerged, and is imposible to walk along the river bank. Frequently, for bathers, matters are exceedingly difficult, and the bathing has to take place at the ends of the narrow lanes abutting on

to the river. Sometimes the water reaches the railings running round the Manikarniká Kund, covering the main part of the old Tárakeshwar temple. Or to give another concrete illustration, the water may be found flowing over the platform of the temple standing right above Dasáshwamedh Ghát.

56. *Lál Ghát or Pakká Ghát.*—A quite unimportant Ghát.

57. *Gáe Ghát.*—There are two flights of steps included in Gáe Ghát. On the northern flight close down by the river there is a very large stone symbol of Mahádeva with a snake coiled round it, and on the same platform about forty similar symbols, but smaller. A still larger symbol of Mahádeva is found on the southern ghát.

58. *Náráyan Ghát.*—Only the remains of the steps exist, the lower part has been entirely swept away.

59.* *Golá Ghát.*—"Gola" means a *market*, especially a market for grain, and this ghát acquired its name through its being the landing place for the grain taken to a market above the ghát. The remains only of the steps are now found, but some pious individual is now having the ghát rebuilt. This part of the city is certainly not too well off for bathing gháts.

60. *Trilochan Ghát.*—Called also *Pilpillá tírth,* "Tírth" means a place of pilgrimage. This ghát and the temples above are about the most sacred corner in this part of the city. In bygone days this portion of the city must have been the most populous and famous, but gradually the city has grown away in a southernly direction, and carried much of its sanctity with it.

Trilochan means "three-eyed," and is a name given to Shiva. The story of the acquisition of this third eye by Mahádeva is a striking illustration of the childishness of many of the stories about the gods, contained in the sacred scriptures of the Hindus. A stronger adjective than *childishness* must be applied to many of the stories. The story runs that Shiva was on one occasion receiving worship from Vishnu, who daily offered up to him exactly a thousand flowers. While Vishnu's attention was, for a moment, diverted, Shiva, in mere playfulness, (one may presume), slipped away one of the flowers. When Vishnu was concluding worship he found that nine hundred and ninty-nine flowers had been offered. What was to be done that the offering might be complete? Vishnu plucked out one of his eyes to be offered in the place of the missing flower, this eye he affixed to Mahádeva's forehead, and there it remained. Thus henceforth Mahádeva possessed three eyes instead of two.

Mr. Sherring, in his book on Benares, at pages 97—103, gives a somewhat full account of the group of temples at Trilochan.

61. *Tiliyá Nálá.*—There is no stone ghát here, but the place is worth noting because of the walls of an old masjid which have fallen quite close to the river. From the name of this old masjid the ghát has been sometimes called "Saqa Ghat." Nálá is frequently applied to the bed of a stream, the flow of which is intermittent. There is a nálá running into the Ganges at this point. It certainly cannot be called a stream, and to speak of it as a sparkling brook might be regarded as irony. The Ganges is attributed with the wonderful power of receiving into her ample bosom boundless defilement, both physical and moral, without herself becoming defiled or contaminated. Well if it is so, for her powers to accomplish this are put to the test very severely in both departments.

A little distance up this nálá is the ruin of another old masjid. At one time this must have been an important Mahommedan centre.

62. *Nayá Ghát.*—" Nayá " signifies *new*, and naturally must have been appropriate to the ghát at some

time. But that must have been long long ago. New Ghát is clearly not the most appropriate name for it now.

63. *Prahlád Ghát.*—This ghát has also traditions connected with it. It stands far away from the modern centre of the city, but has not lost all its ancient renown. It is still regarded as a place of much sanctity.

It is the last of the stone ghâts belonging to the city proper. Prahlád, after whom the ghát is named, is the hero of many stories in the sacred history of India. One of these stories is often portrayed in the sculptures of the temples. Prahlád was the son of an exceedingly wicked but very powerful ruler named Hiranyakashipu. Prahlád, under the instruction of the Brahmans, became a most devout worshipper of Vishnu, and greatly enraged his father by his devotion to the god. Hiranyakashipu resorted to many means to cure the son of his pious ways, but all were in vain. The son would not be restrained from his passionate devotion to Vishnu, and even in the presence of the father loudly hymned the praises of his chosen lord. On one occasion Prahlád had been angering his father beyond measure by telling him that Vishnu was everywhere, even in him, the wicked Hiranyakashipu. The father in great wrath asked, pointing to a stone pillar, "Is he in this pillar?" "Yes." "Then I will smite him," so saying Hiranyakashipu struck the pillar. Immediately the pillar split open, and Vishnu, in a form of half-man and half-lion, came forth from it, and seizing the blasphemous ruler, made short work of him. This picture of Vishnu in a cleft pillar is often found depicted, and sometimes very realistic representations of his rending the wicked Hiranyakashipu.

64. *Ráj Ghát.*—There are here no stone bathing steps, but mention must be made of the ghát as it was a very important crossing before the bridge was built. It was on the Grand Trunk Road, but this latter has been now

diverted so as to connect with the Railway Bridge. The writer well remembers his first entry into Benares over the old Bridge of Boats at Ráj Ghát. There was a certain charm about this comparatively primitive method of entering the ancient city, but it was not all charm, the dust and confusion, the noise and delay, had to be debited on the other side. The charm of crossing the river in the Rainy Season, when there was no bridge of boats, had many mitigations. One used to "drop" across the river only too literally, for the boat would be swept down the river by the strong current, and had to be towed up the other side.

CHAPTER IV.

TEMPLES, TANKS, AND OTHER PLACES OF INTEREST.

THIS chapter is commenced with fear and trembling, for it seems difficult to tell where it may end. Benares teems with places of interest and there appears no special reason why this chapter should not ramble on for a hundred pages or so. Much that is really interesting in Benares must pass unnoticed.

It may perhaps be well to group the places somewhat according to locality. This will make it possible for a visitor to take a group at a time, or he may take special ones from different groups and see as many of these as possible in the time at his disposal. No attempt is made to map out time, as so much depends in this matter on the observer. Some people "do" Benares in a day, others "get a peep at it" in two or three days. In an old guide book an interesting morning's programme was sketched out, and then the remark made "the visitor will return to the hotel to a late breakfast." Late breakfast forsooth! Should the visitor have gone through the programme laid down for him he might be thankful if the supper were not cleared away at the hotel.

It should be stated that some of the places mentioned in this chapter would not prove particularly interesting for a visitor to *see*, but it was felt that they ought to obtain mention, as real interest attaches to them.

1. *Kabír Dás ká Mandir.*—This is situated in a back lane not far from the Municipal Office, in Kabír Chaurá. The property covers a considerable space of ground. On one side of the lane there is a large open court-yard with various buildings round it, a place for the "mahant," or head of the akhárá, and in a chamber are treasured the "gaddi"(the cushion against which a teacher leans), and sandals which belonged to Kabír Dás. In many of these so-called Reformed Sects of Hinduism the worship diverted from idols has a tendency to devolve upon the "guru" (teacher), past or present. This part of the monastery is occupied by devotees belonging to the sect, they may be continuous residents or visitors from other parts. In the court-yard are also some "samádhis" or tombs of deceased mahants. Most mahants and swamies are buried (in the ground or in the river) not cremated. On the other side of the lane there is a garden and a few small buildings. This part is apparently used as a guest-house and here married men with their wives may be accommodated. In this sect all teachers and fully initiated members must be celibates, but lay members need not be so. The two parts of the premises are connected by a small bridge passing over the lane, but they have also their separate doors.

2. *Kabír Dás Ká Baithak.*—This is situated at Lahtárá, some distance away, but as it will not fit in with any other group, and has to do with Kabír Dás it is mentioned here. It lies just outside Benares near the Grand Trunk Road in the Allahabad direction, very near to the 423rd milestone. There is a neatly built temple on a bit of slightly elevated ground to the south of the road,

and above a shallow but wide-spreading tank or pond. It was on this pond that Kabír Dás, as a babe, is said to have been found; hence the veneration in which the spot is held. In the temple, or "mandir," as they prefer to call such buildings, is a "páduká" (footprints) of Kabír Dás, or as his followers often speak of him "Kabír Sahíb." There is apparently only one old Kabír Dásí living at the place, a courteous old fellow, but quite unread, and not knowing much about the history of Kabír Dás. A few graves of deceased devotees are found in the adjoining ground.

3. *Jágeshwar*—This is a small but important temple near to the Ishwargangí Tank. It is on raised ground above the roadway. There is an outer court, with several shrines, and an inner court, containing a large symbol of Shiva. The temple is of no great beauty, nor does it wear an appearance of antiquity, but it seems to enjoy some reputation, and is frequented by the well-to-do. During a recent visit it was found that the wall of the inner temple was under repair, and still more recently it was observed that a central entrance is being made, hithereto it had to be entered by a small side door. These facts are noted because it is rather unusual to see such repairs and improvements being effected in old temples. To repair old temples and tanks brings small reputation, so they are generally left to the wear and tear of time, and new ones are built which will perpetuate the name of the builder.

4. *Pátál Puriyá Sthán.*—This is next door to No. 3, but has no direct connexion with it. Outside the wall are a few Mahommedan tombs, also the very much damaged figure of a—Is it a lion? let us say—of an animal. Within the enclosure is accommodation for about ten sádhus. These sâdhus claim to be Vaishnavites. There are one or two temples or shrines with images of

Shiva, Hanumán, and others, but the special feature of the place is a small opening in the earth, which is said to have no end, that is, not in this world. It is said to lead to Pátál, *i. e.*, hell. Why this spot should be regarded as sacred, and why the entrance to this road to Pátál should be so carefully kept under lock and key, as though people might be trying to effect an entrance surreptitiously, one fails to understand.

5. *Ishwargangí.*—This is a large tank, the age of which is beyond all computation. There are very many places in Benares which have existed from eternity, but this is older than them all. The place possesses no very special interest in spite of this its great age, and is not greatly frequented by bathers. A near resident confessed to me once that in the hot weather when the water gets low, bathing in it is not pleasant, and as he made the remark he gave a most significant shrug. Looking at the water, I believed him. Such a remark is probably applicable to other tanks besides Ishwargangí.

At the four corners of the tank, and at one or two other points, are shrines containing the images of various gods. Among others there is one of the Ganges, represented by a crocodile, and another of the sun. To the east of the tank is a small group of buildings occupied by devotees, whose special deity is Rám. A portion of the Rámáyan is said to be read, or rather chanted, every evening.

To the west of the tank is a rather pretty garden and a temple of the Napalese style of architecture. The garden and temple are both private.

6. *Bará Ganesh.*—Not far from Ishwargangí, to the north of the main City Road, is an interesting group of shrines and temples, the chief of which is one dedicated to Ganesh. On the gateway of nearly every

temple there is a figure of Ganesh, just as on the title page of most Hindi books there is a picture of him, and the first word in the book is an invocation to Ganesh, seeking his blessing on the undertaking. Thus Ganesh shares in the worship offered to all the gods. But here he has the throne and not merely the entrance-hall. The figure of Ganesh is very well-known, a seated human figure, very corpulent, with the head of an elephant possessing only one tusk. Ganesh is reputed to be the son of Mahádeva and Párvatí. Various accounts are given as to how he came by his elephant's head, some of them little to his credit.

In the temple is a very large central figure of Ganesh, parts of which are said to be made of silver. Other smaller figures of the god are found in various parts of the temple, the court-yard, and the verandah. In the verandah is also a very large image of a rat. The rat is always represented as the chosen steed on which Ganesh rides. Considering the portly figure of Ganesh one is disposed to say " rough on rats." The front wall of the building is also ornamented with quite a colony of rats, brillia tly painted. Most of these have their hats on, presumably meant to be crowns.

The temple is modern, but some of the images appear to be of considerable age.

Close by is another temple to Hanumán. The walls of the enclosure in which this temple stands have a touch of antiquity about them. It may be that the stones are old, but the wall far more recent.

In a lane leading to these temples is a small hall or shrine containing the images of a celebrated trio, Jagannáth, Balabhadra, and Subhadrá, or to use their other names, Krishna, his brother Balarám, and their sister Subhadrá. The figures hardly suggest the " three graces." They not only lack beauty of features, but are deficient also in some limbs, though this fact is concealed by the long flowing garments in which their figures are swathed. The faces are brilliantly painted, and evidently every endeavour is made to make them look their best.

7. *Briddh-Kál.*—This lies north-east from the Municipal Gardens, and is another of the very ancient, and very sacred, places of the very holy city. There clearly is a look of antiquity about it, which, bricklayers and house-repairers have made no endeavour to conceal for many a long year. There are several court-yards, but they are in a ruinous state. In different directions are sundry shrines and images, but *the* special object of interest is a small basin or tank, some five or six feet across, the water of which is said to possess marvellous virtues for healing diseases, such as leprosy, etc. There is a well close by, the water of which is to be drunk. By drinking from the latter, bathing in the former, and the exercise of faith (and, of course, making the necessary offerings) great things may be expected.

Tradition hath it that very very very many years ago an old and infirm rájá visited the spot, and gave himself up to a life of ascetic devotion. Mahádeva, being much pleased with this manifestation of piety, granted health and renewed youth to the ancient rájá, and he, in his gratitude, built this sacred place in order that other afflicted ones might obtain the benefits which he had received. Briddh-Kál means "the fate of old age." The place is not much resorted to except on mela days. Somehow faith in the healing powers of the pool at Briddh-Kál does not appear to be very widespread.

8. *Mrityunjaya or Alpmriteshwar.*—This is a small temple containing a symbol of Mahádeva, situated only a few yards to the west of Briddh-Kál. In the centre of the temple (really a small room) is a square cavity or

square basin, in which stands the symbol. By the side of this chamber is another which forms an anteroom to the shrine itself, though there are also wide open windows in the shrine which enable the passer-by to see the god without entering the temple. Though the temple is so unimposing in size there is an air of affluence about it, very different from its near neighbour Briddh-Kál. The steps and the floor of the anteroom are of marble.

Mrityunjaya means "victory over death," the other name, Alpmriteshwar, probably signifies "Lord of the death which overtakes us so early." And yet deaths are not uncommon in Benares. It is marvellous how feeble stern facts appear to be in the presence of hoary traditions, until the fact overtakes the individual.

Another name given to this god by the vulgar is "Bhatkhouwa," *i. e.*, the eater of rice; this name has been applied because rice is offered to the idol.

9. *Alamgir's Mosque.*—This is situated in a back alley about a hundred yards to the south of Briddh-Kál. It is a spot of considerable interest to the antiquarian, for the pillars are evidently very ancient, and are supposed by some to be Buddhistic. They are clearly of a far earlier date than most of the stone carving seen in Hindu temples. It may well be possible that they were first in a Buddhist temple, and after the demolition of that, used in a Hindu temple, this was in its turn destroyed and the pillars built into the present masjid. The pillars are good specimens of early Indian architecture before boldness of design, simplicity, and finished workmanship gave way to elaboration of detail and loss of simple grace.

The Hindu temple which this mosque replaced is still a fresh tradition, the image of the God has been re-established in a temple a little further south. Hindus still visit the old site, and though not allowed to enter the mosque, can gain access to the courtyard, and there they make offerings of flowers to a small stone pillar in the middle of the "hauz" or tank. This, however, has not the slightest relation to Hinduism, being the tank which it is usual to place before a mosque, in order that the worshipper may perform the appointed ablutions before reciting his prayers. The pillar in the centre is probably treated as a Mahádeva by the Hindus, as it does bear some resemblance to that symbol.

On the west side of the courtyard is the mosque, on the south side has just been fixed up a hosiery manufactory. Several very modern knitting machines are here busily at work turning out socks and stockings of good quality, excellent workmanship, and some of them simply gorgeous in pattern. And yet 'tis said that East and West shall never meet.

10. *Krityabáseshwar and Hans Tírth.*—Krityabáseshwar was formerly enshrined in the temple on the site of the present Alamgir mosque, it now finds lodgment in a well-built temple situated a little to the south, on a platform elevated above the road, which has a neat little garden in front of it. Krityabáseshwar signifies "clothed with an elephant's hide," and is a name given to Mahádeva owing to one of the incidents in his long and eventful career.

Immediately at the back of the temple is a tank known as Hans Tírth. A few years ago this was a huge dust and rubbish bin, and a disgrace to any city. Quite recently, however, some public-minded or devout citizen has, at considerable cost, built high brick walls up three sides of the tank. This certainly greatly improves its appearance, but the impurity of the water does not appear to have been greatly mitigated, and is apparently so bad that people do not bathe in it. It seems to be a stagnant pool into which rubbish has been flung and accumulated for many a long year.

On the road between Alamgir's mosque and Krityabáseshwar Temple may be observed two red temples standing close together. One of these is known as Ratneshwar, and contains an image of Mahádeva. The other has figures of Hanumán (the monkey god), and Mahádeva. There is a story that a certain official, many years ago, wished to remove the temple because it impinges so greatly on the road, but he had a vision and desisted from carrying out his intention. Considering the multitude of temples in every direction, it is a matter for wonder that a piece of straight road has ever been made. There are many places besides this where temples impinge on the road or lane (notice a road parallel to this to the west), but perhaps not quite so assertively.

11. *Arhái Kangúra kí Masjid.*—This masjid lies at a little distance off the main road to the Ráj Ghát Railway Station, on the left-hand side. How it came by its name is not clear. Arhái means two and a half, and Kangúra means a dome. On the upper part of both the doorway into the courtyard, and on the centre of the masjid itself are carved two small Kangúras and half of one. These, however, were probably carved to signify the name af the mosque, and are not the cause of the mosque being so called. It is possible that there was on the same site, before the present mosque was built, one that had three domes; in the course of time half of one of the domes fell, and the musjid became known as "the two and a half dome mosque." Later on a new mosque was built but the old name lived on, although the present mosque has but one Kangúra.

The building is rather a fine one, and interesting by reason of the fact that it appears to be largely built of materials which belonged to earlier edifices, either Buddhistic or Hindu, or both. The pillars are certainly not modern. The two large round corner pillars at the back of the masjid should be noticed, as they are quite unusual in such buildings.

Mr. Sherring (pp. 310 ff.) gives an interesting account of a slab in the building bearing the date 1191, and evidently taken from an earlier Hindu building of some kind.

There are numerous groups of temples lying to the right-hand side of this Ráj Ghát Station Road, between it and the river, but we dare not attempt a description of them, they are so numerous. Some slight mention of a few has been given in chapter III.

12. *Ganj-i-Shahídán Mosque.*—This small masjid is one of very special interest owing to the very fine carving on its pillars, and the evident antiquity of these pillars. Apparently this masjid was only re-discovered something like fifty years ago. The ground at this spot was very much higher than it is now, and the masjid was below the level of the ground, and so remained buried. It would seem that the property round the site belonged to a Mahommedan gentleman. One day his servant noticed a hole in the ground. It was surmised that some chamber must be under this, (thus accounting for the sinking of the ground), possibly a treasure chamber. Excavations were started, and the present masjid was unearthed. The name Ganj-i-Shahidan indicates that it was supposed to be the resting place of a great multitude of those who had died for the faith.

There are sixty pillars, including the pilasters. Those to the north of the "mimbar" or pulpit are shorter than the rest and are all of one pattern. The others vary in their shape and carving. Some few have evidently had the carving deliberately chipped away, probably because of figures carved on them which were considered inadmissible in a Mahommedan mosque. The carving on the pillars is very fine. Some of them are suggestive of the period which many regard as Buddhistic, others appear to be of a somewhat later date, a transition period when simplicity was giving way before the tendency towards more elaboration, but still the style might be called classical. The carving of the roof above the puplit is worth noticing.

13. *Ráj Ghát Fort Plateau.*—The two gateways on the north-east of this plateau give unmistakeable testimony to the existence of a fort here in days gone by. Probably this was the centre of Benares at one period of its history. Other ruins point no less distinctly to there having been a time when the south-western portion was a place of considerable importance, held by Mahommedans.

The ground offered natural advantages for a fort, and was probably a strong citadel in its palmy days. It should be realized that in the olden days fort and palace if not absolutely identical were close united. The palace was the centre, and must necessarily be surrounded by a fort for protection.

The ruins about the spot have not been well preserved, on the contrary many things have contributed to effect their effacement. At one time it was occupied by English troops (I recently met an old soldier who remembered staying there). Then during the construction of the Ganges Bridge it became the quarters for the staff. Later on again the Indian National Congress and Exhibition used the ground. Naturally at all such times the ground would need to be levelled, and old bits of ruin would be broken down.

One fine mausoleum (Mahommedan) yet remains, the fine enamel work of which is interesting. There are also parts of two small turrets and the remains of the wall which connected them. These represent the Mahommedan period. The two old gateways already referred to probably belong to an earlier, and Hindu, period.

The buildings connected with the Barná Sangam belong to this plateau, and will be mentioned in the next section.

14. *Barná Sangam.*—Barná Sangam means "the meeting of the Barná (with the Ganges)." The place is supposed to possess great sanctity. It is too far from the city to be much frequented, but at times great concourses of people assemble to observe some special festival. Quite recently the rush of people was so great at a bathing festival that some people were drowned. The spot is important for the pilgrims on the Panchkosí Road, as it is the last place on the return journey before again entering Benares, and special ceremonies have to be performed here.

High up on the bank above the river is a small group of temples, whose reputation has probably somewhat waned, and they fail to attract many worshippers except at mela times, and then the *chief* attraction is the bathing at the junction of the two rivers. There is a special idol of Mahádeva, which, on account of the place, bears the name of Sangameshwar. A somewhat unusual grouping of gods occurs here, there are gathered in one spot images of all three members of the Hindu triad, Brahmá, Vishnu, Mahesh (*i. e.*, Mahádeva). Four-faced images of Brahmá are found here and there but are by no means so common as the other two, they are in fact, relatively, rare. Brahmá in said to have possessed five heads originally, but to have had one cut off by Shiva.

15. *Lát Bhairo.*—This is on the outer road on the way back to Benares from Barná Sangam, on the

right-hand side soon after crossing the Bengal and N. W. Railway line. Hinduism and Mahommedanism are here found in close, and, as it has proved more than once, dangerous proximity.

There is a large tank, in a somewhat dilapidated condition, at which a mela is sometimes held. At such times worshippers come and bathe in its not too tempting water.

The pillar called Lát Bhairo has had a stormy history. In the days of its first glory, apparently, it was enshrined in a temple, but this was destroyed by Aurangzeb and a mosque built on the site (or near it). For some reason or other, however, the column was allowed to remain and this still continued to receive the worship of the devout Hindus. In 1809 there was terrible strife between the Hindus and Mahommedans, resulting in much shedding of blood, and attempts, on both sides, often successful, to defile and destroy the sacred places of the foes. The Hindus burnt the mosque at Lát Bhairo, the Mahommedans retaliated by throwing down, and probably breaking, the sacred pillar of the Hindus. Some say that they flung it into the Ganges. The probability, however, seems that it was overthrown and badly broken, and that after things had quieted down, the pieces of the pillar were collected, and encased in copper as the Lát stands at present.

There are scattered Mahommedan ruins about the spot, and one little place which is carefully kept in order by them for worship, while the Hindus no less carefully guard their sacred emblem

16. *Nág Kuán.*—This is situated to the south of the road leading to the Benares City Railway Station. It is not particularly easy to reach as there is no important road leading to it. This "Snake Well," for such is the meaning of "Nág Kuán," is a singular place, and one

wonders what was the special purpose of the builder of it. There is a very large square platform, about five feet in height, and on mounting this you look down into a wide and very deep pit, the perpendicular walls, or the steps of which are strongly built of stones. Flight of steep steps of various types of break-neck pattern, descend to the bottom of the pit, in one corner of which is the well itself. This is reached by another short flight of steps. The well is not used for ordinary purposes, but once a year a large mela is held at the spot, bathing takes place, and the nág or snake is worshipped. A few other images are found about the platform and steps. Apart from the time of the annual mela the place wears a most woe-begone look, and is allowed to remain in a very filthy condition.

Referring to these steep steps it is a point worthy of notice that Indians have remarkably good nerves with regard to dangerous steps and heights. From childhood they are used to going up and down steps, and walking along ledges that would turn an ordinary European giddy.

17. *Bakariá Kund.*—This lies to the south of the City Station, and lying round it will be found much that is of great interest to the antiquarian. Mr. Sherring devotes a chapter to Bakariyá Kund and its surroundings, and describes the ruins with considerable detail. It is now more than forty years since his book was written, and probably these years have made distinct differences to some of the raised terraces.

We cannot venture upon more than a short notice of the principal buildings. The Kund or pond is a fairly large body of water in the rainy season, but in the hot weather is much reduced in size.

The buildings now to be noticed are situated on the south side of the Kund. Immediately to the south are three masjids, within the enclosures of which are a number of tombs. These masjids are on fairly high ground and there were stone steps leading down to the water. Many of these steps remain, but the mortar has perished and the steps are in a very disordered state. In the stone foundation walls of these mosques may be noticed some slabs of handsomely carved stone which manifestly came from some more ancient buildings. On the platform of the westernly masjid is a solid stone short column with holes cut out all round; this was evidently a "chirághdán," *i. e.*, a lamp stand for holding tiny little open oil lamps such as are still used by the people, though they are fast being discarded in favour of kerosine oil lamps.

In the centre masjid are eight pillars which are decidedly very old. The back four are very deeply carved, and may belong to the earliest period of architecture of which specimens exist in Benares. The front four are octagonal at the bottom, then sixteen-sided, and above that perfectly round. The capitals of the whole eight are massive and have little ornamentation.

In the eastern masjid are four old pillars; all four are alike in shape, *i. e.*, square, but three are perfectly plain, one has a little carving. The entrance doorway to this mosque is very striking. The carving is not particularly deep, and its sharpness has been taken off by successive coats of whitewash, but it is beautiful in its strong outline, and real artistic conception and execution. It suggests the simple strength of the Buddhist period. At the top of the archway is some stonework of a very much later date, and distinctly Mahommedan.

To the south-east of these three mosques is a square roofed pavilion over a tomb. The tomb is Mahommedan, but the four pillars on which the roof rests manifestly belong to an early period. The pillars are square, the lower part is plain, but the upper part, together with the bases and capitals, are very elaborately carved. Some of the details of the carving remind one of the carving on the Dhamek at Sárnáth.

Due west from this, at a considerable distance, is another Mahommedan tomb, but the structure assumes the size of a building. This building is called "battís-khambhá" *i.e.*, "thirty-two pillars." The dome is probably late and has been recently repaired, but the pillars belong to a much earlier period, and are probably in their original position as the architraves are so evidently in keeping with them. There are three porticoes extending on three sides of the central square one, two with four pillars each, and one with two. The "thirty-two pillars" evidently applies to the central pavilion. These pillars are peculiar, each pillar not being a single block of stone, but formed of two or four upright pieces with spaces between them. These separate pieces, however, are united into one pillar by the single base and capital which serves them. These square stone pillars are perfectly plain. Each corner pillar is composed of four stones, the other eight pillars are composed of two stones in each. Thus although there are only twelve main pillars these are really made up of thirty-two smaller ones, and it is these apparently which have given the name to the building.

Apart from Sárnáth, these ruins are about the most interesting in Benares, and excavations would probably reveal much. Excavations cannot be carried out, probably, as the ground has been occupied by Mahommedans for a long time, and there are tombs about in every direction.

To the west and north-west of the battís-khambhá are two finely domed mausoleums to the memory of two Mahommedan saints. There are a few more also to the west of the Kund. Among these latter is a very interesting old tombstone, an oblong, standing about three feet high, and somewhat elaborately carved. According to a reading of the inscription it is about 350 years old.

This ends the first group. "Home to a late breakfast."

The next group of places is contained roughly in a square the diagonal corners of which are the Town Hall and the Observatory. The open space by the Town Hall makes a fine centre for the City. The Gardens are well cared for, and give, with the adjacent open grounds round the public buildings, a splendid "lung" for this congested part of the city.

The Town Hall, the Head Police Station (which might be taken for a fortress), and the Telegraph Office have been already noticed. The Nágarí Prachárini Sabhá Hall, which stands at the corner of the Municipal Gardens, is the head quarters of a Society which has had a long and successful career. It has done much energetic work for the conservation and improvement of Hindi, and is now taking up the very important work of preparing a comprehensive Hindi Dictionary.

At the back of the Gardens is a very oriental garden-house, which belonged to the late Rájá Shiva Prasád.

Immediately to the west of the Town Hall a large temple and other buildings are being erected. These ought to be an adornment to the City, but this possibility will be greatly mitigated, if not entirely annulled, by the builder conforming to a plan, often adopted, of building the ground floor as shops, and letting them out to whatever tradesman may care to take them. This is a form of utilitarianism which makes one long for an Indian Ruskin to arise and address some gentle words to the owners of such properties, suitable to the occasion.

18. *Bhairo Náth.*—The Bhairo Náth Temple is situated in a lane at some little distance from the back

of the Telegraph Office. It is a comparatively insignificant looking temple, but enjoys great popularity. The power of the gods is not to be measured by the size and beauty of the temples they reside in. The upper part of the temple has no chance of displaying itself, as the temple is very much shut in on every side, and has an exceedingly narrow courtyard. Bhairo is regarded as the officer of law and order for Bishwanáth, and it is his duty to keep things generally straight. If he does not altogether succeed in accomplishing such a task it is not matter for wonder. For fulfilling his onerous duties Bhairo Náth is provided with a truncheon, this is no mere badge of office, but a stone implement which certainly ought to strike fear into the hearts of the unruly. There is -something deeply suggestive in the theory which is accepted, that this instrument of punishment becomes self-operative and need not be actually wielded by the hand of Bhairo Náth. It has its seat in a separate temple some distance away. The image of Bhairo is provided with a silver face, near to him is an image of his dog, not the faithful friend, but the steed on which Bhairo rides. The dog thus becomes sacred in all temples dedicated to Bhairo, and dogs in and around them have a good time, being fed by worshippers who visit the temples. These temple-fed dogs assume airs, and sometimes accord the European visitor a welcome, in which respect and fear find small place. The writer has, on more than one occasion, had a lively time, when visiting a Bhairo temple.

Other idols besides Bhairo are found within this temple, and there are some more ancient ones in a lane to the west of this temple.

19. *Dandpán* and *Kálkúp*.—" Dand " means staff, or cudgel, or truncheon, and "pán" equals hand. Dandpán, therefore, means " staff-in-hand," but as we have

seen, the original possessor has trained the staff to do its work without being literally in hand. It is lodged in a temple separately, and has become deified. The staff possesses a silver mask, but this is not commonly worn, it is reserved for gala days. Apparently there is even in India a general acceptance of the fact that if we all had our deserts we should not escape punishment, and so worship is offered up to Dandpán in the hope that the punishment may be avoided or mitigated.

In the same building is Kálkúp or "well of fate." Light reaches the well through a small opening in the wall above the well. The point is for the visitor to look down the well and see the reflection of himself therein; if he does, well and good, it means prosperity and continued life, if not an early death is foreboded. Moral:—Don't pay your visit on a cloudy day, and be sure and ascertain at what hour the light gets the best chance of reaching the water of the well through the narrow opening.

20. *Gopál Mandir.*—This lies just off a narrow but very important and busy lane close to the two temples referred t above. An old-fashioned gateway, and very wide and lofty passage (in which are a few shops), leads to a courtyard on the west side of which the temple is situated. It is on a very high platform, and is not accessible to the European visitor, The courtyard may be approached from the other side by a very narrow passage. From this latter passage is a low covered way leading into a garden. Tulsí Dás is said to have occupied a small house or hut (still pointed out) in this garden. Much difficulty is experienced in obtaining permission to see this, and there is not much to see, when the permission has been obtained.

Gopál (guardian of the cow) is a name given to Krishna (one of the incarnations of Vishnu), especially

THE BRASS BAZAR.

the boy Krishna, as during his youth he dwelt among cowherds, and shared in their duties, going out with the kine to graze them. This temple is exceedingly wealthy, and receives visits from many of the prosperous merchants and bankers of the city. The temple is associated with that section of the worshippers of Vishnu who follow the teachings of Ballabhácharya. His position was that devoutness did not necessitate separation from the world ; the good things of life were to be enjoyed. Few sects have been more loyal to the teachings of their master. Some say that they are unduly zealous in cultivating the pleasures of the material side of life. A Hindu of wide knowledge recently said to me that he believed that Ballabhácharya and his followers had been an unmitigated curse to Hinduism. This side of Hinduism is certainly not its best side, it represents the Hinduism of the Bhágawat Puran as opposed to that of the Bhágawat Gíta.

It will be well to follow this lane along its whole length, passing through the Brass Bazaar and coming out into the main road near the Chauk. The lane is a peculiarly characteristic one. The high houses on either side of the lane, the quaint gateways and doorways, the narrow and crowded thoroughfare, the various commodities displayed for sale,—these cannot but prove of interest to one who wishes to study India, as it is. Here, perhaps, more than in most places, it is possible to study India, *as it was*. Benares is moving rapidly in many respects, but there are phases and features of its life which are distinctly conservative.

21. *Káshi Karwat.*—Leaving the Chauk by a gateway to the east, and then turning sharply to the right, Kachourí Galí is reached, another of the very characteristic lanes of Benares, with its high houses, its eager throngs of pilgrims, its shops with merchandize of very

various sorts, sweetsellers, booksellers, papersellers, grocers who supply spices and dried fruits, picture-sellers, those who sell the miscellaneous articles used in "púja" (*i. e.*, worship),—It is a busy striking scene, to be gazed at keenly and to live in the memory afterwards for many a long day.

In a narrow passage turning off to the right from this lane, is a small shrine called Káshi Karwat. The building is a small one, and covers a well, in which, close to the water is a celebrated Mahádeva. A grating covers the mouth of the well, and the worshippers mostly satisfy themselves by casting a few flowers down the well through the grating, without actually entering the building at all. Inside the building there is a narrow staircase leading down to the well, but this is generally covered by a trap-door. It is only open sometimes.

22. *Gyán Bápi.*—Descending from the lane by a sloping footway the first building that meets the eye is the mosque of Aurangzeb, which replaces the old temple of Bishwanáth demolished by the Mahommadans. It is a fine building, though not greatly used, and has always been an eyesore to Hindus, established as it is in the very centre of what they regard as peculiarly holy ground. It was at this spot that the quarrel arose in the year 1809, which proved so disastrous.

At the back of the mosque and in continuation of it are some broken remains of what was probably the old Bishwanáth Temple. It must have been a right noble building; there is nothing finer, in the way of architecture in the whole city, than this scrap. A few pillars inside the mosque appear to be very old also.

To the east of the mosque is situated a plain but well-built colonnade, covering Gyán Bápi, the Well of Knowledge. This well is surrounded by a stone screen, at which sits a Brahman. The worshippers come to the

The Well of Knowledge—Gyan Bapi.

well, make their offering of flowers, and receive from the hand of the Brahman a small spoonful of water from the well; this they apply to their forehead and eyes, and some of them drink a little, and then go away enlightened and wise. Oh! the sadness of it. But is there not such a thing as "holy water" in Europe?

To the north of the colonnade is a huge figure of a bull, the steed of Mahádeva. This bull is regarded with much veneration, and is freely worshipped. In the hot weather a punkhah is fixed above its head, and worshippers can give a pull at this, and thus render service and give a whiff of comfort to the object of their worship. It is surprising, however, that the punkhah has been so badly fixed, that each swing not only creates a draught, but knocks the bull on the head. This is peculiarly lacking in, not only reverence, but ordinary decency. Imagine a servant hitting his master on the head at every swing of the punkhah!

Close to this bull is a shrine with figures of Gaurí Shankar, *i. e.* Párvatí and Mahádeva.

In this same open space there are one or two other small temples and a large figure of Ganesh, suitably placed near the well of knowledge for Ganesh is the god of wisdom.

23. *Temple of Bishwanáth, or Bishweshwar, or the Golden Temple.*—From the eastern side of the space in which Gyán Bápi stands, a narrow doorway leads into an equally narrow passage, which running by the side of the Golden Temple joins the lane on to which it fronts. Close to the doorway should be noticed a blind alley which contains a large collection of images, especially of symbols of Mahádeva. The European visitor is not allowed down this alley, but a view of much of its contents may be obtained from the end of the alley. What a collection of images it is! One of the strange features

of idolatry is the enormous multiplication of the idols, especially, in Benares, of these symbols of Mahádeva, each one of which is supposed to possess such untold efficacy.

This assemblage of images is spoken of as the court (legal) of Bishwanáth. One division is called the civil court, the other the criminal. In the former is a life-size figure of a certain Nandá Brahmacháry, a saint of long ago.

Entrance to the courtyard of the Golden Temple is not accorded to those who are not Hindus. A general view of the interior is obtainable from the doorway. There are three buildings; that to the right is the temple of Bishwanáth, that to the left of Mahádeva Dandpán, the central building is an open hall with a domed roof, and is called "baikunth" (heaven). It will be noticed that there is some very fine carving on these buildings. A better view of the two spires and the dome may be obtained from the first floor of a building right opposite the temple. Flower-sellers occupy the ground floor; no difficulty is raised about a visitor ascending the stairs and getting a view of the Golden Temple. One of the spires and the dome are said to be made of copper plates coated with gold. They certainly present a striking appearance glittering in the sunlight, but the high wall of the courtyard and the straitened space in which the temple stands gives the building no chance to display its proportions. This is true of many of the temples.

As Bishwanáth (*i.e.*, Shiva or Mahádeva) is the patron god of Benares it is not surprising that this principal temple to that deity should be much resorted to. The jostling crowd struggling to effect an entrance, and then an exit, is a sight to remember. The worshipper makes offerings, including flowers and Ganges water, and also rings one of the numerous bells.

Opposite Biswanáth is another Mahádeva Temple, with fine carving. There are two spires, one on the temple itself, the second on the portico. The last is worth noting as it is rather out of the usual, a great number of figures are seated in rows all over it, these are saints meditating upon Mahádeva.

To the east of Bishwanáth is a large temple to Tárakeshwar. Some two hundred yards to the north-west from here, across the main road is the temple of Ad-bishweshwar, which is said to be the oldest Bishwanáth, older even than that destroyed by Aurangzeb. It has a somewhat ancient look, but there is nothing of special interest to take the visitor there. In spite of its claims to antiquity it is not attractive to pilgrims, they swarm off to the modern rival.

24. *Annapúrana Temple.*—Passing along the lane from the Golden Temple, Annapúrana is found on the left-hand side. Several temples intervene but they must pass unnoticed here. A long line of beggars sits along the front of the temple; this community is not unrepresented elsewhere in Benares, but they are in special evidence here as the traditions of the temple rather play into their hands. Annapúrana is the Hindu "Copia," who, with her Cornucopia meets the needs of all. Annapúrana is specially deputed by Mahádeva to supply the inhabitants of Benares with food. The goddess is enthroned in the central building, other gods are lodged in the verandah round the courtyard and receive the worship of the devout. This temple is sometimes called the cow temple, on account of the number of cows and bullocks which wander about the temple and are fed by the worshippers.

Immediately beyond this temple, as you pass from one lane to another by a narrow doorway, there is a very uncouth figure of Ganesh, with silver appendages. He appears to be very popular, and receives no little attention from the devout who throng past, on their way to the Golden Temple. The special name for this Ganesh is Dhundhráj.

25. *Sákhí Bináyak.*—Before passing along to Sákhí Bináyak it will be worth while to step a few yards along a lane to the right to observe what is called the Gosain's Temple. It is a good specimen of modern Indian sculpture, with most elaborately adorned pillars, the details of which are chiselled with much care and skill.

Retracing one's steps and passing along the lane leading towards Dasáshwamedh, there is on the right-hand side a temple of Sákhí Bináyak, a large figure of Ganesh. Sákhí means "witness," Bináyak is another name for Ganesh. Ganesh is here worshipped as the witness and recorder of men's good deeds. Those who perform the Pánchkosí pilgrimage, always come here at the end of it, that Ganesh may duly record the fact, and secure for them the fitting reward of their meritorious task. In the verandah is a large figure of Hanumán.

On the left-hand side of the lane before reaching Dasáshwamedh is a shrine with a figure of Shankaráchárya, one of the most influential teachers that India has ever had.

26. *Jangam Bábá.*—This spot is some distance from Dasáshwamedh, on the main road leading to Assí Ghát.

The garden of Jangam Bábá is of sufficient importance to have given its name to the mohalla in which it is situated. The title Jangam Bábá is given to the mahant for the time being of the Saivite sect which has a monastery here. There are about a hundred followers of the sect in residence, and there is further accommodation for visitors.

The followers appear to hail largely from the South. The monastery is well endowed, it holds other property besides the valuable property in Benares itself. The sect is specially devoted to the worship of Mahádeva, and each disciple and follower wears a symbol of Mahádeva round his neck.

In the grounds of the monastery are several temples and shrines, also the "samádhis" (tombs) of several of the deceased mahants. The original Jangam Bábá is reported to be still alive in his tomb. The temples here very strikingly illustrate a point already referred to, *viz.*, the passion for multiplying idols. In the various temples and shrines in this one spot there are probably not less than 2,000 symbols of Mahádeva.

We pass now to a third group of temples and tanks. The part of the city to be dealt with is very crowded with temples, and we can but notice a few.

A most interesting walk may be secured by diving into a narrow lane which runs nearly due south from opposite the Fish and Fruit Market at Dasáshwamedh, and extends to the Kedár Náth Temple. For the whole length, between this lane and the river are many many temples, some of them are large temples with images of Mahádeva and other idols; there are numerous shrines, collections of whole and mutilated images gathered together under trees, and odds and ends in every conceivable corner. Probably it would be no great exaggeration to say that in Benares there are as many idols as inhabitants.

27. *Mánsarowar Tank.*—Through a doorway on the right-hand side of this lane, some distance along, entrance may be obtained to the enclosure in which Mánsarowar is situated. It is a deep tank, containing little water during the greater part of the year. There are numerous shrines and images in various directions, especially on the north side, and north-west corner. The whole place is in a most dilapidated condition, and

unless the Mánsarowar Lake, hidden away amid the far heights of the Himálayas, has purer water and more beauteous and sweet surroundings, its inaccessibility is not a matter for regret. The tank is said to have been built by Rájá Mán Singh, whose memory is perpetuated in the Observatory. The play on the word "Mán" here is quite characteristic.

After reaching the temple of Kedár Náth, a tortuous way may be worked out still running parallel with the river, or turning round sharp to the right the main Assí Ghát Road may be reached.

28. *Tilbhándeshwar Temple.*—Not far from the junction with this main road, (to the N.-W., in a narrow lane) stands a celebrated temple with a huge symbol of Mahádeva. This is said to grow a "til" (a small black seed from which oil is extracted) in size every day. What efficacy, as a god, this gradual but ceaseless growth can give to this particular idol is not self evident.

Under a pipal tree is part of a very large image of a man. This figure is now called Bírbhadra, a certain Hindú demi-god, but this is only an adaptation. The figure is so fixed as to appear to be half buried in the earth, but it is probable that nearly every inch of the figure which exists is visible. It is the upper part of the figure, from the waist, and stands some four or five feet high, including the hair which is bound up into a high head dress, one entire arm is broken off, and the hand from the other side. The image is evidently very old and far more akin to the Buddhistic age than to the Hindu stamp of idols. Close by, built into the side of the platform on which the Tilbhándeshwar Temple stands, there is another figure, probably of about the same age.

About a hundred yards away from this temple, to the south-west, is an old temple called Mukteshwar, and here also is found a figure of apparently somewhat the same period.

29. *Lalárak Kund.*—Passing along the main Assí Road, by turning up a narrow lane to the left, after passing the water-works, Lalárak Kund may be reached. This is a large well and "báwálí." There is an ordinary well, but on one side of this a huge excavation has been made, down the three sides of which, away from the well, are three steep flights of steps leading down to the level of the water in the well, and as there is at that point an arched opening in the wall between the well and the Báwálí, the water in the well can be reached by descending these steps of the báwálí, and there is a small tank formed at the bottom of the báwálí where the three flights of steps meet, and into this the water from the well flows, when it is tolerably high.

The place is deserted and neglected during the greater part of the year, but an annual mela is held during the rainy season, and then crowds of women flock down the steps and bathe in the water. After doing so, they go to the Ganges (which is very near), and bathe there also, and this seems a sensible plan, for in such a little used and neglected well, the water can scarcely be regarded as ideal for bathing purposes.

Somewhat further on, to the right of the Assí Road there is another curious báwálí, of another pattern, with steps leading down to the water. Adjoining this is an enclosure containing two or three temples, and some quaint paintings are found on the verandahs.

Near to this point is a narrow road running to Durgá Kund and the Monkey Temple.

30. *Kurukshetra Tank.*—On the left-hand side of this road is a new temple which has already been noticeed in Section 1 of Chapter III. Nearly opposite this, on the other side of the road, is a large tank, which bears the

name of Kurukshetra, the celebrated battle-field referred to so often in the Mahábhárat. The surroundings are in a neglected condition, and the water scant and far from clean. To the north and north-east of this tank are several monasteries belonging to the Nának-panthís, who are strongly represented about this part of the city.

31. *Mausoleum of Swámi Bháskaránand.*—In a garden to the left, immediately before reaching Durgá Kund, dwelt for many years an old devotee, by name Bháskaránand. If he possessed great learning he had the humility to conceal it. He lived a life of simplicity, even unto nakedness, and was very clean and amiable. Upon what his great reputation depended I know not, but a reputation he certainly enjoyed, and many Hindus came to the garden and worshipped "the holy man." He accepted such worship with an easy grace. Even during his lifetime a small temple was erected in the garden, in which a marble image of the Swámi was enshrined. He died some few years ago and was buried in the garden. Two of his admirers are now having erected a very handsome mausoleum over his remains. This is said to be costing some £ 8,000. It is a beautiful piece of work, the most beautiful of its kind in Benares. It is constructed of pure white marble throughout, except the floor of the platform, which has squares of a darker shade of marble. The design is full of grace, and there is no excess of ornamentation, what carving there is, is simple and beautiful in design and execution. In years to come it will probably be regarded as the gem of architecture in Benares.

32. *Durgá Kund* and *The Monkey Temple.*—No attempt will be made to give an elaborate description of these places, this has been very much overdone already by other writers. There is a large tank, the water of

TOMB OF SWAMI BHASKARANAND
(*Unfinished*).

which sadly needs a bath itself in the hot months, when the water runs low. Adjoining the tank is a temple, before which goats are sacrificed. The temple is a very ordinary one, of no great beauty. Monkeys infest the temple and its neighbourhood, and when not being fed by the devout visitors to the temple, make life an anxiety for the people who live near. Their sacred associations have not delivered the monkeys from their natural propensities for thieving. The monkey is reverenced in India because this was the form in which a god and many demi-gods became incarnated and helped Rám in his fight against Rávan, the demon king of Lanka, *i.e.*, Ceylon. The king of these monkeys was Hanumán, son of the Wind, who did marvels of prowess and strength in the service of Rám. Hanumán or Mahábir is much worshipped, and many are the images of him to be found in Benares and elsewhere.

33. *Lakshmí Kund.*—This tank lies north of the road running west from Daśáshwamedh Ghát. It has well-built stone steps, and a fair supply of water. The tank was cleaned out a few years ago, but even after that the water is not all that might be desired. There are some temples on the north side. That which gives its name to the tank being one in which Lakshmí, the goddess of wealth, is enshrined. It is rather strange to see an English clock over the inner door of this shrine.

About the month of August or September a mela is held here which lasts for a fortnight. This is not only a bathing festival, but becomes a fair, and Lakshmí Kund presents a busy scene, especially during the last few days of the mela.

There are a few stones lying about by the tank, which are elaborately carved, and apparently came from some ancient buildings.

34. *Súraj Kund.*—This is situated north-west from the above. Súraj Kund means Tank of the Sun, and is so called from a figure of the Sun in a small pavilion-like temple near to the tank. The Sun (called Súraj or Súraj Náráyan) is much worshipped, chiefly in his natural form, but also under symbolic form carved in stone. In various places in the city these symbols are found. There are a few other images in and around the temple, but of the place generally it may be said that its sun has set. There are two flights of steps to the tank, but there is little water, and what there is, is mud.

35. *Pitar Kund.* (The Tank of the Fathers).—This is situated not far from the large Aurangábád Serai. There are stone steps on two sides of it and a good supply of water. The tank is much used for bathing by those living in the immediate neighbourhood. Originally the place was much frequented for the purpose of making offerings for deceased ancestors on the father's side, but apparently with changing times these ceremonies have been transferred to Pishách Mochan Tank.

There are three Shiválás (temples to Mahádeva) above the steps on the east side of the tank.

36. *Mátá Kund.*—This lies almost immediately to the west ofPitar Kund. The name means "The Tank of the Mothers," and here were made offerings for ancestors on the maternal side. Poor mothers and their relatives! The tank is little better than a cesspool, and there are only ruinous traces of a flight of steps.

37. *Pishách Mochan Tank.*—This tank has a past, and even now enjoys great popularity. The pristine glory of the flights of steps has long since been dimmed. Those to the north and south are very much broken, and in many parts non-existent. Those to the east are in a better condition, and the majority of buildings are on this side of the tank. There are sheds in which visitors

Head of the Pishach at Pishachmochan Tank.

go through the ceremonies for their ancestórs, and also several temples. It is on the platform of one of these that the pisháčh's head is placed, of whom more anon. There is another good-sized temple on the south, and a few little shrines and temples hither and thither in the immediate neighbourhood of the tank.

There is, of course, a legend about the pisháčh or goblin, from whose hands "mochan," *i. e.*, deliverance is here sought. The legend runs that once upon a time a very fierce demon attempted to force his way into the sacred city. He overcame the guardians stationed on the outskirts, and reached this spot. Here the demon was tackled by Bhairo, who after a fierce struggle conquered the demon and cut off his head. The beheaded, but not extinct, demon humbled himself before Bhairo's master, Bishwanáth, and obtained permission to still dwell on the spot where he had been overcome, on condition that he would allow no other demon to enter the city. He also obtained the further boon that pilgrims proceeding to Gaya, to perform worship for their ancestors, should call here and worship him. And there is the head of the goblin to vouch for the truth of the story. The expression on his face is heavy rather than fierce, though benignity is altogether absent, and deliverance from such a being is clearly to be desired.

38. Here this chapter must close, though there are many places of interest left unnoticed.

There is an old well called Dharm-kúp, near to Mír Ghát, and several old shrines and pieces of sculpture near it, which are well worth examining.

The Rájá of Amethi's Temple, situated near Manikarniká Ghát, seems greatly to have captivated the artistic eye of Mr. Havell, and it certainly is a fine structure, and in a fine position.

The almost disused tank of Karanghantá, near to the Town Hall, will repay a visit, to the curious.

Elsewhere the temples of Kámeshwar and Bágeshwar and many another "eshwar" (eshwar, from íshwar means god or lord), are to be found.

Little mention has been made of the Jain temples, of which there are over twenty in and around Benares. Some by the Minarets, others by Tulsí Ghát, one by the Vizianagram Palace, another by the Town Hall. There is another at Sárnáth, and the prettiest group of all in a garden about a mile from Sárnáth.

Benares is full of interest to those open to be interested, and volumes might be written about the temples, and tanks and the traditions connected with them. But there are other important subjects connected with Benares, and these must receive some attention.

Ramnagar Fort

CHAPTER V.

RAMNAGAR.

RAMNAGAR Fort is the residence of His Highness the Maharaja of Benares, and is well worth a visit. Of course, entrance into the Fort and Palace can only be obtained by special permission, but even apart from that, the drive to the river is a very delightful one, and there are one or two objects of considerable interest which may be seen without any special permit.

From Cantonments it is a drive of some four miles, by the route detailed in Chapter II. On reaching the Ganges, Rámnagar stands right opposite, and presents an imposing appearance. The various groups of buildings which compose the Palace are high above the river, and are supported by very solid walls which rise from the river bed. These walls are unbroken, except for the stairway, which leads into the Palace by a fine doorway.

It has already been explained that this was not the original seat of the Benares Rájás. Rájá Balwant Singh forsook Gangápur in about 1750, and choosing this magnificent site built the present Fort. Much, however, has since been done to improve both it and the adjoining town of Rámnagar. His son, Rájá Chet

Singh, continued the work, and built the very fine tank and temple about a mile from the Palace.

Should the visitor have obtained permission to see the Fort, he will probably enter it, not from the river, but from the Rámnagar side.

In the Fort there is an Armoury containing interesting specimens of weapons of days gone by. The reception room is a fine oblong hall, having on its walls paintings of the present and former Mahárájás. There are some good specimens of fine carved ivory work, carved, I believe, in the palace, which have replaced far less effective ornaments. This is a happy indication of the efforts now being put forth in some quarters, to revive indigenous arts and industries, and to let pure Indian art take the place of tawdry European trinkets.

Leading from this hall is a fine balcony with marble floor and a very handsome marble throne. From this balcony a magnificent view of Benares is obtained.

There are several temples in the Fort, one being in honour of Vedavyás. a great saint of ancient days, to whom well-nigh innumerable books are attributed. To Vedavyás is also attributed a very gracious boon granted to the dwellers on the Rámnagar side of the river. The tradition runs that he was on his way to Benares, but having reached Rámnagar, was so delighted with it that he would proceed no further. There was the tradition that to die on the Rámnagar side of the river Ganges was to suffer great loss and shame in the next birth, but Vedavyás instituted a pilgrimage by which this disaster might be averted, and a great annual mela is still held, which is said to have thus originated.

One hesitates to mention another treasure of the Palace, as permission to see it can only be obtained under very special circumstances. This treasure is an illuminated copy of the Rámáyan of Tulsí Dás. Probably

SUMERU TEMPLE AND TANK AT RAMNAGAR.

there is not in the whole of India a work of the kind that exceeds this in interest and beauty. The whole is beautifully written by hand in the Nágari character, and each page has an illuminated border, and is faced by a full page painting depicting some incident described in the text. The whole work is bound into five volumes, in Indian style, not in leather, but in artistic Kinkáb-work.

About a mile from the Fort there is an exceedingly fine tank, on the side of which is a garden and garden-house, where the Mahárájá sometimes entertains his European friends.

On another side of the tank is a lofty temple visible from afar. The four sides are adorned with very elaborately carved figures of animals and gods. The workmanship is undoubtedly fine, but taking the temple as a whole, it is more remarkable for wealth of detail than for real beauty of architecture, it seems to lack strength and symmetry.

Inside the temple are images of Shiva, Durgá, and other gods and goddesses.

A possible way of return (if previous arrangements have been made for a conveyance) is by the east side of the Ganges, crossing it by the Dufferin Bridge.

The present Mahárájá has proved himself a loyal and warm friend of the English, and by his courtesy and generosity has won many warm friends.

CHAPTER VI.

THE RELIGIOUS LIFE AND SIGNIFICANCE OF BENARES.

IT is quite clear that in attempting to deal with this phase of the life of Benares we must concentrate our attention on those features of it which appear to bear on the general tendency of the religious life and destiny of the people of Benares and of India. Much must pass unnoticed, which, though deeply interesting, does not appear to have important bearings on this.

It is on this ground that we propose to pass over the Mahommedan community, numerically strong though it be, constituting about one quarter of the population. In thus passing it over there is not the slightest implication that the Mahommedans are an unimportant factor in the general life of Benares. This is far from being the case. From the industrial standpoint, they are *very* important; in the Courts (and litigation looms large in Indian life) they are quite prominent and efficient; in civic life, moreover, they are taking their full share. Yet to one living in, and familiar with, Benares, there comes the strong feeling that in trying to grapple with the religious life of this city of Káshi, and to read its significance, the Mahommedan section of the population does not mean all that the number of its followers might naturally lead one to expect, who approaches the question from the outside. There are very many evidences that they are not heedless of the religious side of life but what they are, in this respect, they are, mainly, in and for themselves. They are fairly much what Mahommedans are in hundreds of other places in India, there is nothing peculiarly characteristic about the Mahommedans of Benares, no great movement among them, or power, which indicates that they are likely to alter the religious life of the city, or of India. Their religious life may be much to them, it is not greatly significant as regards the religious life of India for the future. In other words, in making a study of religion as presented in Benares, there is nothing outstanding in its manifestation here, nothing which suggests that we have special opportunities of studying it in its special character, and its influence on the world around.

It is quite different with Hinduism, the whole place is impregnated and saturated with it. Not only does it meet the eye at every point, but it appears to dominate well nigh everything. That Benares is a distinctly Hindu city is not a fact to be deduced from a study of the statistical tables, and the discovery that about seventy-five per cent. of the population are Hindus; rather is it a conviction carried home to the mind by a consideration of the totality of the life of the city, in its many and varied elements.

Jainism is another element which may be left out of our study. The community is small, prosperous, and (judging by the number of their temples in comparison with the number of Jains), religious. But here again there is the feeling that what they are, they are to and for themselves; they are not to any appreciable extent influencing others, or even contributing to the development of their own religion in any special way.

What has to be said about Christianity will be said in a separate chapter.

Having thus cleared the ground to some extent, we will endeavour to examine the religious life of the city, and to gauge its tendency and significance. Hinduism is here used in its very broadest possible meaning, and will include the various movements which either sprang from it, or are still more or less closely identified with it.

The first question which naturally suggests itself is :—What is Hinduism essentially ? It might be thought that Benares would afford unusual opportunities for obtaining an answer to this very important question. In one way it does : the great variety of beliefs and practices found among those who connect themselves with Hinduism, and who are in a general way regarded as Hindus, help to reduce the answer to our question to narrower limits, by shewing some of the things which are *not* regarded as essentials of Hinduism.

In many religions the statement is made that the creed confessed must be judged as a creed, and not by its followers who may be greatly lax and inconsistent, that the creed gives the essentials of the religion. There is doubtless a measure of truth in this, though not the whole truth. But clearly this could not be the standard by which to measure Hinduism. In the first place, there is no creed to set forth its essentials. Again, there is probably no religion in the world which is so tolerant of a variety of beliefs. Identity of practice, again, cannot be said to constitute the essence of Hinduism, for it is perfectly evident that divergencies in the practices of the religious life are very great, though it is likewise true that considerable uniformity of ceremonies is found among large sections of the community, here, again, however, we must note that there are large sections among whom such ceremonies are not regarded as binding. In its final issue, does it not resolve itself into this? Wide divergencies of belief may be allowed, differences of conduct (even ethical) may be permitted, ceremonials may be put on one side, the broadest interpretations of the sacred books may be practically if not formally sanctioned, every doctrine of Hinduism may be questioned, *but* a general loyalty to the corporate body of Hinduism must be looked for, and a measure of conformity required to the attitude of that section of the corporate body with which the adherent is identified. Just as in Indian law there are many cases relating to marriage, adoption, inheritance, etc., for which there is no universal standard, but that which is regarded as the law in the community to which the man belongs is accepted as the law by which that man's case must be decided; so, in Hinduism, there is no universal standard, but loyalty to Hinduism must be estimated by a general acceptance of the standard and rule of that section of Hinduism to which each one may belong. The ordinary rules of caste are quite ignored by many of the devotees belonging to some of the innumerable sects which exist within the pale of Hinduism, and yet these devotees are regarded as Hindus, and are frequently supported by Hindus not because they are poor, but because they are leading the religious life. Hinduism is neither a creed, nor a church, nor a society with unalterable rules and regulations, but a loose federation whose only uniting bond is a general consent, expressed or implied, to an undefined brotherhood of sympathy, and loyalty to an unwritten tradition that "we are all one body though differing so greatly." This is not a satisfactory definition of Hinduism, it is vague in the extreme, but it is certainly not more vague than the facts which it is sought to define.

It is difficult to say how far the members of the various reformed sects, such as the Arya Samáj, the Bráhmo

Samáj, and others would be regarded as having a claim to be called Hindus. Some of them have certainly forfeited their rights, but it would appear that they are under no such stigma as those who should embrace Mahommedanism or Christianity. Probably it is fair in speaking of Hinduism broadly to include all these various sects, though dou tless some of them are under many disabilities and are not in full standing.

Taking this inclusive view of Hinduism, its composition is very mixed. Many sects are represented in Benares.

The Arya Samáj exists here, though it is neither very strong nor very aggressive. It is a protest against many of the modern corruptions of Hinduism, especially against idolatry. It would make the Vedas the sole standard of creed and pratice. It is, so to speak, a severe legalism, harking back to first sources, and protesting againt the traditionalism and vagaries of the forms which modern Hinduism has assumed. This sect has a hall (not yet completed), on the main road between the Town Hall and the Chauk.

The Bráhmo Samáj is decidedly weak in Benares, but is not unrepresented. This is an eclectic sect, which without entirely breaking with all the traditions of Hinduism, claims the right to choose the best of all the creeds, and to break away from the corruptions, in creed and practice, of Hinduism, wherever they appear faulty. The history of this movement is one of great interest, but does not belong to a description of Benares. Those who desire to read a good account of the movement will find Mr. J. Campbell Oman's book "The Brahmans, Theists, and Muslims of India" a most readable and helpful work.

The followers of Kabír Dás have an important centre in Benares. Their monastery is situated in Kabír Chaurá Mohallá. Kabír Dás was an eclectic, and his one endeavour, to teach a monotheism which all might hold, though expressing it in various ways. He was neither a Hindu nor Mahommedan in his teachings, and yet at his death was claimed by both. He protested against idolatry, pronounced the spirit of religion to be more important than its form, and the name by which God was called a matter of comparative indifference, so long as God was really worshipped. He taught the necessity of a good life and the broad spirit of brotherhood, insisting on these points as of far greater importance than any mere outward orthodoxy. The guru or teacher was exalted to a position of great authority, so much so that in course of time the guru has, to a large extent, assumed the status which the Brahman possesses among the orthodox. Celibacy is insisted on for full disciples of the sect, but not for those who are adherents. In other words, it is necessary for the clergy, but not for the laity.

So few Dádupanthís are found in Benares that it is not necessary to devote any space to an account of the sect. Very broadly speaking it is a collateral sect working along the same lines as the Kabírdásís.

The Nánakpanthís have a considerable following in Benares. They have akhárás, or monasteries, round about Assí Ghát and Kurukshetra, Mír Ghát, the Chauk, and near the Bisheshar Road grain market. They are the followers of the Punjabi, Nának Sháh. The teaching of Nának Sháh accords in many respects with that of Kabír Dás and Dádu Diyál. It involves a somewhat loose monotheism, the spirit of brotherliness of mind and act, and general worthiness of life. These things were made to be the essentials of religion. That which was started as a religious union grew, by force of circumstances, into a political confederacy, the Ṣikhs, but it is with the religious movement that we have to do. There are different sub-sects among the Nánakpanthís, two of them are represented in

Benares, the Udásís and the Nirmalís, (the "Mendicants" and the "Pure"); these appear to be on good terms with each other, and at times share a common meal.

Concerning this sect, more perhaps even than concerning the Kabírdásís, the remark should be made that there is a constant tendency for them to get away from the teaching of their founder, and to drift back towards ordinary Hinduism. They study many of the Hindu sacred books, in conjunction with their own, and get more and more involved in the distinctive teachings of Hinduism. There may not be actual participation in idolatry, but there is nothing like the strong protest against it that was put forward by the founder of the organisation. The Granth, or book, which contains the teachings of Nának Sháh (and probably much of those of his successors mixed with them), is accorded a place of peculiar honour in their places of worship, and something dangerously akin to worship of the book is prevalent. Possibly the worship of gurus and books is hardly less dangerous than the worship of idols.

The Gorakhpanthís have a large building close to the Municipal Gardens, and another about half a mile away, but the residents of the two akhárás are not apparently very closely connected. In Benares the followers belonging to this sect are few. Gorakh Náth, the founder of the sect, has been very much canonized, so much so that now his followers say that he had neither birthplace nor grave. It is not only Gorakh Náth, however, that they worship. In the principal akhárá there are several temples and shrines with symbols of Mahádeva in them, and these are, apparently, freely worshipped. They probably try to identify Gorakh Náth with Mahádeva, making out that Gorakh Náth was a manifestation of Mahádeva.

The Nágás have three akhárás in Benares, representing three different sub-sects; two of them are side by side in the buildings above Shiválá Ghát, and the third at Hanumán Ghát, immediately to the north. There is not much protestantism about this sect; they did protest against some of the conventions of life, such as clothes, but have had to give in on this matter. They constitute, with their sub-divisions, another of the almost innumerable sects within the pale of more or less orthodox Hinduism.

There are other sects, such as the Raidásís, the Shiva Náráyanís, the Dasnámís, and others which have nothing very distinctive in their doctrines. They are all probably more or less remotely descended from Rámánand, who was, in a sense, the father of the Kabírdásís, Nánakpanthís, and numerous sects akin to them. The three sects mentioned above, the Raidásís, etc., have extended largely among the lower caste people, forasmuch as they protest against caste, and substitute gurus, taken from among themselves, instead of from among the Brahmans. Commonly the reverence accorded to the guru is great, but in the practical outworking of the system, and the system is well organised, the "panchayat" (call it committee) imposes a distinct limitation on the guru's power over the community. These sects commonly possess a sacred book all their own; but it is often a compilation from kindred literature, or else vague and illiterate versification composed by men who have had little education, and are not born or trained theologians.

These sects, however, play no unimportant a part in the lives of very many of the people. Kept aloof by the caste-Hindus, they are enabled to take something of an independent stand, and to feel that they are a community, and the teachings current among them, and their organisations, are not without some moral influence on the lives of those who are members of the communities.

It is worth noting that some of them have adopted

burial instead of cremation in the disposal of their dead.

One other sect must be noticed, the Rádháswámís. This sect* is of quite modern origin, but has grown rapidly in several towns in the United Provinces. The sect was founded by a certain Shiva Dayál Singh, a well-educated man, who died only some thirty years ago. In more recent years Pundit Brahmá Shankar Misr, a member of a particularly clever and respected family in Benares, took a leading part in the movement. He was a man of considerable ability, and threw his whole energies into the development of the sect. Taking long leave from his Government appointment, he settled down at the "Mádho Dás' Garden," which he had acquired some time previously, and started building a very imposing looking hall for the religious uses of the Rádháswámís, and was also devoting himself to literary work in connection with the sect. At the time he was in delicate health, and was overtaken by death before either of his tasks was accomplished. The building has since been finished, (costing some Rs. 60,000) and is quite a modern structure in style, with iron girders and pillars, and a gallery, built especially for the accommodation of women. The building is said to be capable of seating 2,000 worshippers. The "holy ashes" of the late revered guru are deposited under a sort of altar, in the centre of the raised platform at the north end of the hall. Some of the furniture which he used is treasured up also, in the way of relics, and the way is being prepared for the sainting of the deceased, if not his deification.

To describe the tenets of the sect is not easy. The guru was not eager to expound them to any one who was not willing to join the sect, and would plainly say that they were incomprehensible except to the initiated. There is much that is esoteric, and much that is mystical about the teaching. Apparently an attempt has been made to graft some psychological science, of a very unproved character, upon some of the teachings of such men as Kabír Dás and others. Much is made of the "shabd" (word, sound, *cf.* logos). Yogic practices are encouraged, and much importance is attached to the buzzing sounds in the head which may be thus produced. To the uninitiated, the system presents a strange mixture of mysticism and pseudo-science, but to the initiated appears far more than this. Apparently the guru is placed in a dangerously giddy position. Spiritual principles rather than a personal God appear to be prominent in the teaching.

The sects already mentioned seem to be on the fringe of Hinduism, whether strictly within the pale or not is not easy to decide in many cases.

But what about Hinduism proper? What exposition can be given of that? There are such innumerable divisions, doctrines, practices, that probably no one could give a comprehensive account of them all, and such a full account would probably find few readers.

There is the old-fashioned "Shástrí," the man learned in Sanskrit lore, deeply conservative, and accepting, to a large extent, the whole body of the Hindus' sacred literature, though allowing that there are different phases of teaching, adapted to different stages of men's development; philosophical speculations for the learned, crude idolatry for the uneducated masses. Then there are the family priests, and other orders of Brahmans engaged in similar duties, men who are not greatly learned, but have memorized the formularies necessary for the performance of the various rites and ceremonies. The Pujárís are associated with the worship in the temples, and are generally learned in little except the formalities connected with the care and worship of the idols, and the receiving of offerings. There are the Gangáputrás (sons of the Ganges) who have charge of the bathing gháts.

But quite apart from these professional classes of Hinduism, there are to be considered the many Hindus who have no professional interests at stake, and are therefore less prejudiced witnesses as to their real beliefs. Many belong to the respectable body, to be found in every religion, who jog along the well-beaten path, give a nominal assent to all that their fathers believed, and observe more or less strictly the various rites and ceremonies. There are others who have advanced a stage, they are readers, possibly thinkers; many of these hold very loosely by idolatry, and maintain that "knowledge" is the great means to salvation. Among this group many Vedántists are found, the great majority in Benares following more or less closely the Shankaráchárya or Adwait School, *i.e.*, holding that the world and man are but passing phantoms and dreams, the only reality being God. Their great doctrine is expressed in the sentence "There is one (thing)—God, there is naught else." This sentence is sometimes translated "There is one God, there is no other," and made to imply that the teaching is monotheistic; but this is not so, this is to lose the whole point of the teaching of Shankaráchárya, which is Monism of the severest type, and not Monotheism. Among the Vedántists are men of various shades of thought. Some give up the severe Monism of Shankaráchárya, and incline to the type of Vedántism taught by Rámánuj and his successors, who accord more or less personality to God, and seek to save men's personality. There are not a few who are seekers after truth, realizing that they have found no sure resting place. Agnosticism counts many followers, men who have broken with Hinduism mentally, but have reached no other position. Idolaters vary greatly; there are many who go through the prescribed performances, not greatly believing in them, but not sufficiently interested in spiritual matters to have reached the stage

Some Holy Men.

of unbelief. Then how many genuinely devout idolators there are, men and women who honestly believe in all that their spiritual guides have told them, and implicitly do what they are bidden. There are many who have given up belief in idolatry, and the stories connected with it, and yet are nominal adherents. "Do you believe these things?" "I shut my eyes and believe."

An important feature of the life of Benares is the large opportunity afforded for Brahmans coming from different parts of India, being supported at the Chhatras, gaining instruction in the formularies of Hinduism, and possibly a smattering of other Sanskrit learning, and then returning to their own country to be the teachers, and priests of the people. Some of course, get more than a smattering of Sanskrit learning, they become really learned pundits.

These Chhatras mentioned above require a little further notice. They very in their scope and purpose, but, unitedly, embrace the uses of hostels, scholarships, and alms-houses. By endowments alone, provision is made for the support of over two thousand persons, it has been recently stated, four thousand. This provision is not exclusively for Brahmans, but much of the money has been left explicitly for them, and they possibly get their full share of the endowments not thus limited. In some cases there are buildings where Brahman students can be accommodated, more commonly the endowment arranges for a daily dole to the recipients.

About Sádhus, so-called devotees, perhaps the less said the better. There are Sádhus and Sádhus. Some are only lazy, some are vicious. Many among the Hindus themselves are getting more and more to feel what a weary load these men are upon the country, and how demoralizing to the whole community. This system of religious vagrancy is inevitably bound up with the views about the "renunciation of the world" which find so large a place in Hinduism. Somehow the people who renounce the world shew no eagerness to renounce food, some of them, by their appearance, must have exceedingly good appetites. Their demands from the hard-worked and under-fed people are a disgrace and a shame. Why should these thousands of lazy fellows live a life of absolute idleness while others have to work the harder to keep them going?

One other special feature of the religious life of Benares demands notice, *viz.*, the visits of enormous numbers of pilgrims. For the local festivals the throngs of people who troop in are mostly from the adjacent villages, but at the more general festivals, and especially at the time of eclipses, hundreds of thousands come from afar. Quite apart also from these special occasions, there are continually coming those who are "on pilgrimage," and, of course, Káshí must be included in the programme. These hundreds of thousands of pilgrims are a source of no small gain to the residents of Benares. The tradesmen reap considerable benefit, and of course the Brahmans are not the poorer. Some of the pilgrims are rájás, and other wealthy men, and spend great sums of money in offerings and so-called charities. While these pilgrimages bring so much financial gain to the city, who can measure the religious demoralization that is continually being effected.

Still another special feature of the life of Benares remains to be noticed. Very many people come here to die. Some of these are men of position, Government officials who have retired, and others, who retire and come to the holy city that they may spend their last days here, die within the sacred precincts, and have their ashes cast into mother Ganges as she flows by the city consecrated to the god who gave her birth. Not a

Bathing Scene.

few widows also come to spend their last years here. It may interest some to know that some of the temple authorities make an annuity arrangement with widows who desire it. The widows make over to them such money as they possess and are then entitled to subsistence as long as they live.

Among the religious influences which are at present operative in Benares no mention has been made of Theosophy, which has made the city its head quarters for this part of India. So far as Theosophy has become identified with the life of Benares, it has become an interpretation of Hinduism. Doubtless, however, it brings much from the West, and endeavours to read it into Hinduism, and in this way is influencing Hinduism. Ethical teaching nurtured and developed by Christianity, and incorporated into the life and thought of the West, is read into the Hindu shástras, and taught as Hinduism. It may be freely granted that much of the teaching may be found in the Hindu books, but never focused and enforced as it is being now done through agencies which are, in their sources, distinctly Christian. This statement may not pass unchallenged, but it is written thoughtfully and deliberately.

This is a very imperfect sketch of the variegated religious life of Benares. The question now suggests itself—What is the significance of it all? Benares is often spoken of as a conservative centre of Hinduism, but is this the case? Conservatism there doubtless is. There are not a few whose conservatism can be respected, though we may not agree with their position, the conservatism of those who are wedded to the past, and who are convinced that what has been established from of old must be right. There is the conservatism of those who "love to have it so," whose bread and butter it is. "But you know these things are not right, why do you allow and encourage them?" "What can we do, where is our food to come from if this be given up?" This conservatism is not rare, alas! in Benares.

But Benares is by no means wholly conservative. Liberalism, both of views and practice, are growing. Progress, distinct progress there is, even though it be not so fast as many would wish. The material progress is quite evident, and it ought to be, in common justice, mentioned that the splendid services rendered to the city by Government officials has had much to do with this. The city has been favoured with Collectors and Commissioners during recent years who, backed up by the Municipality, have been able to carry on real progressive work in the way of improvements in the City. For many years, we enjoyed the services of Mr. E. H. Radice, as Collector, and Mr. D. C. Baillie, as Commissioner, and probably never did officials enjoy such popularity as they did, secured by their hearty sympathy with the people, and their readiness to work for, and with, them. There can be no doubt but that this had much to do with the loyal spirit that pervaded Benares during the recent days, when there was so much "unrest" present in various parts of India. But we are not dealing here with such matters.

What is the religious outlook? In the first place, it may be truthfully said that the religious life, even when most closely identified with idolatry, has never sunk to the depths which have been reached in some other parts of India. But when the best possible has been said, the idolatry of Benares is such as to cause deep pain and sorrow to every high-minded well-wisher of the city. The idols must number tens, perhaps hundreds, of thousands. Their coarseness needs no description, this is evident to all who have eyes to see, and the still coarser stories about these gods, contained in the

Puráns, which are reckoned as sacred books, only increases the wonder that such gods can ever call forth worship.

But this is only one side of Hinduism, there is another side, the so-called "Higher Hinduism." It is to be greatly regretted that on the part of these more advanced Hindus there is not a greater effort to sweep away idolatry from the masses, and to give them something in its place. It may be that many, lost in the subtle metaphysics of the Vedánta, feel that they have nothing to offer, which is capable of being appreciated by the common people, no simple Gospel, easily understood of the unlearned, and capable of influencing their lives towards higher things. And yet, be the sources whatever they may, changes are being effected, there is gradually wrought into the spirit of very many an altered attitude towards the things which belong to the moral elevation of a people. Things can never, we trust, drift back to where they were, or even remain as they are. Quite recently has been issued a book, by a Hindu, which speaks in no measured terms of many of the evils of Hinduism, and pleads earnestly for their being removed. Another resident of Benares could be mentioned, a man of great ability, who takes a similar attitude, but who cares not, or dares not, to speak out in the same way, and it is so with very many others. There are many men, well educated, thoughtful, whose moral nature revolts against the baser features of Hinduism, and would fain see things greatly changed.

In closing this chapter, therefore, the writer's last word is one of hopefulness. The City is not even now *wholly* given to idolatry, and it may be that in the future Benares may be worthier of its name of Káshí, the Illustrious City.

CHAPTER VII.

CHRISTIAN MISSIONS.

IT would naturally be expected that such a city as Benares would make a strong appeal to those who believed that God had laid it upon them to carry the Evangel of Jesus Christ to India. Such a centre and fortress of Hinduism would suggest to them what Jericho suggested to Israel of old, though in another sense, *that* was the geographical key of the land, *this* the key of the Hinduism of, at least, Northern India. Many more than seven days have passed, and the walls have not yet fallen down flat, but Christ's servants still compass the city, sound their trumpets, and "hope on hope ever." The work of renewal is greater than that of destruction, we need not wonder if it take a longer time.

We find that Christian Missions have been established here for only little short of a century. The Baptist Society started work in 1816, the Church Missionary Society in 1817, the London Missionary Society only three years later, in 1820. In 1867 the Zenana Bible and Medical Mission (then called the Indian Female Normal School and Instruction Society) took up work here, in 1878 the Wesleyan Missionary Society. There is a Roman Catholic Chapel, and a resident priest, but as this work lies mostly, if not entirely among Europeans and Eurasians, it does not come within the scope of this chapter.

The Baptist Missionary Society was the first to enter the field, and worked on until 1890. It then decided to concentrate its forces, and seeing that other Societies were occupying the field, withdrew, and strengthened its Delhi Mission. It, however, left one lady worker, who, with her assistants, has been carrying on work among the girls and women. The Mission used various agencies, Schools for both boys and girls, preaching, and Zenana work. Orphanages also were established.

The Church Missionary Society has a large and important work. There is a large Girls' Orphanage, and it is reckoned that since its establishment between 2,000 and 3,000 girls have been trained and educated. Another special feature of their work is a well-organised Girls' Boarding School, with which is incorporated a Training School for Teachers. The large Boys' School in the City was endowed by the late Rájá Jai Náráyan Ghosal. There are also one or two smaller schools for boys and girls. A special form of work is undertaken by the Rev. J. J. Johnson among the Sanskrit Pundits, a work for which he is peculiarly fitted as he is himself a profound Sanskrit scholar.

The London Missionary Society has been engaged in Educational and Evangelistic work. Both Boys and Girls' Schools have been very vigorously carried on, and Evangelistic work is sustained in the City and District The Rev. M. A. Sherring, one of its missionaries, accomplished some valuable literary work.

The Zenana Bible and Medical Mission for some years confined its activities to Girls' Schools and Zenana work, but in 1887 started a Medical Dispensary for women. In 1888 was built the Victoria Hospital, a thoroughly well-built and well-equipped Hospital. This is situated near Sigra, they have also a Dispensary in the City. The Hospital reports, for last year, an average number of in-patients of 43, and out-patients at the Hospital Dispensary and at the one in the City 4,454, with 10,430 attendances.

The Wesleyan Mission has worked on general lines, but recently they have been developing work among the Doms and other low castes, and are seeking to raise them spiritually and socially. This special work among the low castes has been a feature of Mission work in South India for many years, and has become increasingly so in North India more recently. It is a form of work which has raised much discussion. Some have regarded it as a "small profits and quick returns" policy, but it should be regarded from a far higher and broader standpoint than that from which such an estimate of the movement is obtained. If Christianity mean anything, it means God's love and care for all men, and the uplifting of the "depressed classes" of India (oppressed classes would be a still more suitable term) is utterly in a line with Christ's teaching and example. The fruits of this work are wider even than the benefits to the classes themselves. One most desirable result that it is producing is to create a conscience on this matter among other classes of Hindus ; they are being shamed into a recognition of the claims which these oppressed classes have upon their sympathy and help. One Society has been formed among the Indians themselves, in West India, to carry on work among these classes, and it is candidly confessed that the Society sprang into existence through the influence of Christianity. From many quarters now are heard from among the Indians themselves the plea that these neglected low caste people are members of our common humanity, and that it is the duty of all to seek their help and uplifting.

The five Missionary Societies working in Benares have altogether 8 Boys' Schools, with over 1,000 pupils, 18 Girls' Schools with only a few short of 1,000 pupils, and over 900 pupils, in 630 different private houses (Zenana pupils.) There are thus about three thousand boys, girls, and women coming under Christian instruction. In addition to this there are in the Zenanas many who, though not pupils, are brought in contact with the teachers, and come directly under Christian teaching. The English ladies are aided in their work by a large staff of Indian workers, and more is being done than in former years to make these properly trained teachers.

Not only is Bible teaching given in all the Schools, both for Boys and Girls, but Sunday Schools are held in many places on the Sunday, which are voluntarily attended by the School children.

Possibly of recent years not quite so much importance has been attached to Bazaar Preaching as was the case in earlier years. The work, however, is steadily carried on, and *should* be carried on, for, by it, a class of people is reached who are not so likely to come under the influence of Christanity in the Mission Schools. Preaching, moreover, is not only instruction and information, but an endeavour to stir up to activity and effectiveness the knowledge of spiritual things which may already be possessed.

Another form of Christian work which should not pass unnoticed is that of the distribution of the Scriptures and Christian literature. Dr. Charles Baumann, of the C. M. S., started a Bible and Christian Book Shop in 1894. The first item which appears in the books, on the receipt side, is a donation from "a Christian coolie" (*i. e.*, a labourer) of Rs. 100. A poor man bequeathed this sum for the circulation of those books which had brought such blessing into his own life, and thus led to the establishment of the Bible Depôt. On Dr. Baumann's death in 1897, the Book Shop was established on a broader basis, and has since been managed by a Committee representing all the Missionary Societies working in Benares. The Chaplain of the English Church is also a member of this Committee; and in this and other ways the Chaplain for the time being invariably identifies himself with the work of the various Societies. Denominationalism is not so rampant out here as it is at home, men and women, representing different Churches, work not only side by side, but in hearty co-operation.

The Book Shop enjoys the advantage of a fine room, or rather hall, favourably situated on the main road by Rámkatorá, placed at the service of the Society by the Zenana Bible and Medical Mission. The work has steadily progressed. The last year's report shewed an income, by sales of Bibles, Christian Books, and stationery, of Rs. 1,081. The number of such Bibles, books, and portions sold was only just short of 9,000, in addition to which many thousands of Christian Tracts were supplied for gratuitous distribution.

Results! Results! This is the half taunting query often brought forward. The Indian Christian community numbers about 800, including the children in the Sigra Orphanage and Girls' Boarding School. Numerically this does not appear to be a great achievement for nearly a century of work. Estimates of the worth of renewed humanity differ; to those who take the heavenly, the angels' standard, spoken of in the Gospels, the fact of eight hundred persons, young and old, confessedly Christian, will afford grounds for deep thankfulness. "But what of the quality of these Christians." "My good friend, what of eight hundred nominal Christians in England? Some are good, some middling, some not quite that. What more could be said in England? And, there are men and women among the Indian Christian community of whom any church in England or elsewhere might well be proud."

To attempt to gauge the value of Mission work by statistics is a very superficial business. The influence of Christianity is simply incalculable. We do well to be eager for results, visible and tangible results, but it is well also to be patient and hopeful. It is impossible to estimate the effect of Christian educational work among the boys and young men, among the girls and women. The constant preaching to willing listeners, the social intercourse with non-Christians are by no means fruitless, though figures cannot be given. The actual Mission statistics represent but a fraction of the achievements of Christian Missions. The numerous movements among the people themselves in matters of social and religious reform, are not these to a very large extent the outcome of Christian work in this country? The strength of a current cannot be gauged by the ripples on the surface of the water, neither can the results of Christianity be estimated by the number of baptisms. The affirmation may be ventured that Christ is working more effectively in the heart and life of many an unbaptised Hindu or Mahommedan, than in some of those whose names are enrolled in Church Registers, both in England and India.

Christian Missions may seem comparative failures to those who have never made the conversion of the nations to Jesus Christ a matter of prayerful concern, but to those who have, while the visible results may bring great disappointment and humiliation, there cannot be a sense of failure. We are neither defeated nor dismayed, or if we are, Jesus Christ is not. The kingdom cometh not with observation, but it surely cometh.

CHAPTER VIII.

EDUCATION.

THE subject of Education demands a short chapter to itself, for not only is the subject very important in itself, but Benares has special features as an educational centre, and this increasingly so from year to year.

No attempt will be made to trace the history of the various institutions, except in one or two cases. The aim will rather be to give a very brief sketch of what is being done at the present time.

No one will dispute the value of education, except the uneducated, though a variety of views may be held as to what constitutes "education," the extent to which facilities should be afforded for the many obtaining higher education, whether steps should be taken to ensure all children getting primary education, whether English should be encouraged, or whether the vernaculars should be more insisted on,——These and many other questions of a similar character are deeply interesting, but the discussion of them would not be suitable here, even had the writer the knowledge to present the various aspects of the questions profitably.

In the first place, let us have a few bald statistics. It is hoped that these are approximately correct, but in obtaining the details for such statistics from various sources, there is the danger of a small school being omitted, or of its being included twice. These returns, however, will be sufficiently accurate to serve the purpose for which this book is being written.

Some of the institutions are under the Provincial Government, some are under the Municipality, others are more or less private schools, some of them, receiving Government aid, have to conform to Government regulations in many particulars, those which do not receive such aid are of course perfectly independent.

The following table gives the numbers of Schools and students :—

	Schools and Colleges.		Number of students.
2	English Colleges	... ...	367
2	Sanskrit Colleges	... ...	448
4			815
1	Arabic School ...	... .	165
6	High Schools ...	... ...	2,136
1	Anglo-Vernacular Middle School	... ...	324
8	Upper Primary Schools	.. ..	953
17	Lower Primary Schools ...	... ...	881
90	Private Hindu Schools ...	... ...	3,175
53	Private Mahommedan Schools	... ...	1,494
176			9,128
180	Schools and Colleges.	Total pupils ...	9,943
	About 26 Girls' Schools	" ...	1,500

The two Colleges are the Government College (Queen's College), and the Central Hindu College.

The two Sanskrit Colleges are departments of the above two English Colleges, the latter, however, has a distinct name, being called the Ranavír Páthshálá.

The Arabic School mentioned by itself is the Madrasa Mazhúr-ul-alúm, this is by no means the only Arabic School, but being an aided School appears separately.

Of the six High Schools, two are Mission Schools, with 730 students. Altogether Mission Schools appear to have about 1,044 boys, and 990 girls under instruction, besides the educational work among girls and women which is carried on in the Zenanas.

The education given in these very various institutions differs greatly. The College and High Schools are thoroughly well equipped, and quite up to date. In these the Vernaculars are taught, also the Indian classical languages, but the main medium of instruction is English. This arises through no endeavour to thrust English forward, but simply in response to the eager demands of the Indians themselves, who realize the many advantages for their future prospects which the acquisition of English will secure for them.

In many of the Primary Schools the education is necessarily of a very limited character. Some of the boys may afterwards enter other Schools and go on to something better, but naturally many of the parents cannot afford this, and the boys have to face life with some idea of the three R's, but this is a distinct gain.

What can be said about the Private Schools, the Hindu "Páthshálás" and the Mahommedan "Maktabs?" In some of them doubtless more or less sound work is done in Sanskrit and Arabic, in some others there is simply the memorizing of Sanskrit and Arabic, a training for the memory it is true, but this can hardly be called a liberal education. Many of these private schools are carried on under very primitive conditions, in these the Vernaculars, or English, may be taught, but frequently by those who are but moderate scholars themselves, and have little idea of teaching. It must, I think, be confessed that the statement that close on 10,000 students are being *educated* in Benares, is rather a stretch of language. However, they are under instruction of some sort or kind.

The education of girls is a question which is only now being brought into the domain of practical realisation. At present things can only be regarded as most unsatisfactory. In most cases girls who are sent to schools are taken away as soon as they reach an age when they would be able to make substantial progress; they just get through the drudgery of learning the letters, and are beginning to read, when their coming to school is stopped, they are too old to be allowed to leave the privacy of the home. Early marriage is, of course, the main difficulty in this matter. In the Sigra Girls' Boarding School much is being done in the more advanced education of the daughters of Christian parents, and such schools will have a very important bearing on the general progress of the Indian Christian community. The Central Training School was established in the City in the year 1907. It is graded as an Upper Primary School, there are 126 pupils on the roll. The endeavour is to make this a school especially for the training of teachers, and great strides may reasonably be anticipated in this matter during the next decade.

The attitude of the educated towards female education has marvellously changed during recent years, a new era has dawned, which is full of significance, and great social changes must be effected in the near future. A few words must be written concerning the two most recent educational institutions in Benares, the Central Hindu College, and the Hewitt Kshatriya School.

The Central Hindu College has now completed the tenth year of its existence, and during that period has developed in a most remarkable way. Mrs. Annie Besant, the President of the College, has been the leading spirit from first to last, but has had valuable aid ooth in gifts of property and money, and in hearty and efficient service. The School started in the City, but was transferred to its present site in 1899. A valuable property, consisting of land and houses, was given by H. H. the Mahárájá of Benares. The original building has been altered and enlarged, many others have been erected, including Boarding Houses; and now the College and School are splendidly housed and well equipped in every way. As the name indicates, it is for Hindus, and Hindu teaching forms the base of the religious instruction given in the School.

The number of students, according to the latest particulars published, is between 900 and 1,000. Of this number, about 240 are in the College Classes, about 540 in the High School, and about 140 in the Sanskrit department.

There is also a Girls' School, with about 120 names on the rolls. The College and High School are affiliated with the Allahabad University, but do not accept Government aid. An annual expenditure (including addition to buildings) of over Rs. 100,000 is met chiefly by donations, subscriptions, interest on investments, and fees. It was reckoned that during the first nine years over Rs. 1,189,000 had been received, of which somewhere about a quarter had been laid out in building and furnishing, and something less than a half had been invested.

The Hewitt Kshatriya School is yet quite in its infancy, but bids fair to become an institution of considerable importance, not only in Benares, but in the Province. This School is endowed by the Rájá of Bhingá. He gives for its establishment and upkeep Rs. 1,000,000, and in addition to this a fine site of 180 bighas of land, with two large houses on it, and a further sum of

Rs. 150,000 for building. The School has already been started, and has 211 names on the roll, but the work has yet to be organised and developed, and more suitable buildings erected.

The school is specially, if not exclusively, intended for members of the Kshatriya caste, and the Rájá is most anxious that the school should be a nursery for loyalty. Some difference of opinion exists as to the wisdom of drawing the members of one caste into a school by themselves, and thus fostering the caste spirit. Much might be said on both sides of this question, but of the loyal and good intentions of the Rájá there can be no doubt. The institution will greatly increase the importance of Benares as an educational centre, and may, it is hoped, develop into one of the leading educational institutions of North India.

CHAPTER IX.

HAGIOLOGY.

A SKETCH of Benares would be incomplete which did not contain some reference to the saints whose names have been so closely associated with the sacred city. Five are selected for notice, though the notices must be brief. The five are: 1. Buddhá, 2. Rámánand, 3. Kabír Dás, 4. Ballabhácharya, and 5. Tulsí Dás.

BUDDHA.

It seems most probable that Buddhá's real name was Gautama, and from his family name he is called Sákya Muni, *i. e.*, Saint Sákya. Buddhá means "the enlightened one," he also was entitled Siddhártha, *i. e.*, "he who has accomplished man's true aim and end in life."

According to tradition he was the son of Suddhodana, Rájá of Kapilvastu, (about 100 miles north of Benares), and was born about 558 B. C., though there is much uncertainty about the dates of his life.

In his youth he was of a meditative disposition, and though by no means without the accomplishments which suited his station in life, he was more given to quiet and reflection than to the ordinary occupations of a prince.

While still young he was married to a maiden of great beauty, and after ten years a son was born to them. Meanwhile his reflections over the problems of life had convinced him of the vanity of all earthly things. Poverty, disease, old-age, death, these were the calamities that dogged men's lives; what attitude should man take towards a world where these evils reigned? At about the age of thirty he made what is spoken of as the Great Renunciation. Without trusting himself to look upon the face of the new-born babe, or that of his fair wife, he stole away in the dead of the night, rode far from the palace, sent back his horse, assumed the garb of a *religious*, and joining two Brahman ascetics, applied himself to austerities at Rájagriha, in the Patna District. Failing to secure peace of mind, or light upon the problems which perplexed him, he left his companions, and joined by five disciples, entered upon a course of meditation at the spot now called Buddha Gayá. Here after five long years of waiting, and of fierce struggle with the powers of darkness, he received the great "Enlightenment," and rising up, he went forth to proclaim "The Law." It was to the Deer Forest, Sárnáth, that he directed his steps, and there gathered his first followers round him.

What was his message for mankind? He absolutely opposed caste, holding that all men are equal, and capable of obtaining Salvation. This is to be secured, not by ceremonies or austerities, but by following the "Law." The doctrine of Karma takes a very prominent place in his teaching, but the present as an inevitable outcome of all the past was not to be urged as an excuse for supineness, men were to be up and doing. The main essentials of the "Law" which he preached were: 1. Reverence to superiors, 2. Self-control, 3. Kindness to all men, 4. A recognition of the sanctity of all life.

God was not denied, but practically ignored. Karma was a self-working law, needing none to enforce it, nor could it be evaded by the intervention of deities, its course could only be altered by the altered course of each man's life. The end of all was to escape the bonds of conscious existence, to reach "Nirwána," though whether this should be taken as equivalent to absolute extinction, or as being merged in the ocean of life and bare being, is not clear.

Apparently during the remaining forty-four years or so of his life he spent much time at Rájagriha, and still more in wandering about disseminating his doctrines. There is a touching story of his father's acceptance of the new "Law," and of his wife and son becoming disciples. Buddha is supposed to have peacefully died about 478 B. C. after solemnly committing to his disciples the duty of carrying on his great work.

Buddha was greatly original, yet in his speculations owed much to others of a like mind who had been striving after something higher than the current Brahmanism. Budhism, *as a religion,* is dead in Benares, dead in the greater part of India, but it is by no means dead as an influence, and has probably powerfully affected the philosophical side of the Higher Hinduism of more recent times.

It is passing strange that though Benares is the great centre of Hinduism, it should also be so closely associated with the work of Buddha, whose creed now affects the lives of something like fifty millions of human beings.

RAMANAND.

The length of Rámánand's connexion with Benares is by no means clear. There can be no doubting the fact that he resided here for some time, and taught those doctrines, which, through his disciples, have done so much to gather out many sects known as Vaishnavas. These sects identify themselves largely with the worship of Vishnu under his incarnation as Rám, and Rám's wife and brother, Sítá and Lakshman.

Apparently Rámánand flourished about the 14th century. About his exact date there is much difference of opinion.

Rámánuj had broken away from the severely logical and metaphysical Adwaitism of Shankaráchárya, and had infused a measure of warmth into worship and life by his teachings concerning the personality of God, and man's distinct though dependent existence. Rámánand carried this teaching further, and by making Rám the object of devotion and worship, sought to purify and quicken the religious lives of the masses. The long line of Rámánand's disciples has helped materially to direct the religious life of India into healthier channels than the worship of Rádhá-Krishna and Mahádeva, which have done so much to debase India.

Rámánand probably did much to break down the severe restrictions of caste, at least among the Religious Orders founded by him or his successors. The doctrine of "Bhakti" (love of, and devotion to, God), is made much of, is made the essential thing in religion, including love of man, and a good life. Apparently Rámánand was not a great writer, though it is said that hymns attributed to him are still current.

Notice of Rámánand's connection (or reputed connection) with Kabír Dás will be noticed under the sketch of Kabír's life.

As far as I know, there is no building in Benares pointed out as having been the residence of Rámánand, but there is a small covered platform (marhí), just above the river at Panchgangá Ghát, in which, on a raised square of stone or brick is a "páduká" or foot-prints, of Rámánand.

Among the multiplied sects, the followers of later teachers, the name of Rámánand has lost the prominent place which it certainly deserves. Probably the fact that he left no writings accounts largely for this. He is a teacher who has lived in his disciples.

KABIR DAS.

The accounts of Kabír Dás are so various, and so coloured with the marvellous, that it is difficult to arrive at solid fact. The place and date of his birth, his parentage, his religion by birth, whether Hindu or Mahommedan,—all these points are wrapped in much obscurity.

Canon Westcott, in his "Kabir and the Kabir Panth," recently published, has given a very good sketch of the life of Kabír.

Probably he was born about the middle of the 15th century. Some traditions deny him earthly parentage, still more deny him an earthly father. They will have it that his mother was a Brahman virgin widow, who through the benediction of a saint, gave birth to the child. Fearing to face a sceptical world with a son born under such circumstances, the mother forsook him, and he was found and adopted by a Mahommedan weaver and his wife, named Nírú and Nímá. The place is still pointed out, near the 423rd milestone on the Allahabad Road, at Lahatárá (or Lahar táláo) where Kabír was found, floating on the water, on a lotus leaf. Probably he was brought up in his childhood as a Mahommedan, but he appears to have been early drawn towards Hindu teachers, so much so that he was most eager to become a disciple of some accredited Hindu guru. Experiencing difficulty in this matter, he sought to effect his end by a *ruse*. He lay on the path or steps to one of the ghâts at Panchgangá, whither Rámánand came day by day to bathe. Rámánand stepped on the lad, and gave way to the exclamation "Rám! Rám!" This Kabír inferred, must be his mantra, and adopting this for his own, he claimed to have been initiated as a disciple of Rámánand, and the master would not repudiate him.

Thus he would appear to have grown up under the combined influence of Hindu and Mahommedan teaching, and it is very clear that he attempted to combine both.

Probably it is the sanctity accorded to the celibate life which has led to the denial that Loí was the wife of Kabír. She is made his disciple, and the two children, a boy and a girl, named Kamál and Kamáli, to have been adopted children. Kabír is reported to have died at a great age, probably about 1558 A. D. at Maghár, in the Gorakhpur District. Where he spent all his long life does not transpire, probably much of it in Benares, possibly considerable portions of it in Jaunpur, and probably also, he would be much away on long tours disseminating his doctrines.

The estimation in which he was held by both many Mahommedans and many Hindus is evidenced by the tradition that upon his death a dispute arose among Hindus and Mahommedans as to who should have the disposal of his body. While they disputed, Kabír appeared, and bade them lift the cloth from the corpse, they did so, and found nothing but a bunch of flowers; half of these were taken by the Hindus and cremated, the other half by the Mahommedans and buried.

Kabír Dásís, *i.e.*, followers of Kabír Dás, are numerous at the present time, but his real work in India ought not to be measured by the number of his professed followers, but by the influence which his teaching has so widely exercised.

His poetry has been collected, but apparently no attempt to do this was made until a considerable time after his death, and it is doubtful how far the "Bíjak" and other works are the genuine writings of Kabír, and how far the poetry of his followers has been interpolated. Possibly in these verses which are genuine many mis-renderings have become current.

Kabír taught that the question of the name under which God was worshipped was of minor importance, so long as He was regarded as one, and a spirit of devotion towards Him was maintained. Devotion was to displace ritualism, and righteousness ceremonialism. Falsehood and hypocrisy were to be put away, men were to walk humbly before God, and in love one towards another. There is a great deal that is mystical in his writings, and the guru is far too highly exalted. Some of his poetry is exceedingly difficult by reason of this mysticism, and the allusiveness and elliptical style in which he writes. He used the language of the common people, and many of his couplets are full of strong common sense, of much devoutness, and are often very terse and vigorous. In this latter respect probably no Indian writer has ever surpassed him. An English translation of some of these couplets may very suitably close this slight sketch.

1. My Master keeps a shop and plies his trade without difficulty,
   He has no scales, yet weighs the whole world.

2. I am a sinner from my birth, full of evil from head to foot;
   Thou who art the Giver, and the Destroyer of pain, effect my deliverance.

3. A guru is needed who is like a polisher,
   Then the rust of all your births will be destroyed in a moment.

4. Stole an anvil, made a votive offering of a needle,
And then away to some high place, to see how far off the chariot is which is to convey him to heaven.

5. Whatever I have is not mine, it is Thine.
I yield Thee but thine own. What belongs to me ?

6. From one country we came, and landed at the same pier,
But, touched by the world's breath of wind, we travel off on a dozen roads.

7. The place where love dwells not, is just a burning-place (for cremation),
Like a blacksmith's bellows which breathe, but have no life.

8. Book after book is read, but the world lies dead, not one wise man.
Let but the two and a half lettered word "Love" be learned, and then you have a wise man.

9. Penance is not equal to truth, nor is there any sin like untruth.
In whose heart dwells truth, there dost Thou dwell.

10. The work of to-morrow do to-day, to-day's at once.
The end of the world may come in a moment, what will you do then ?

11. In times of trouble all men remember God, in times of joy no one does.
Remember Him in joy. Then, why should trouble come ?

12. Save your head and you lose it, cut it off and you retain it.
Just as when you cut the lamp-wick and make it burn brightly.

13. Everything comes from the Divine Master, nothing from the servant;
From a mustard-seed He makes a mountain, and reduces a mountain to the size of a mustard-seed.

BALLABHACHARYA.

Ballabhácharya's name must be included in the number of those who have helped to make the worship of Krishna and Rádhá (his mistress) widely prevalent. Though not born in Benares, his childhood and education are associated with it; he returned later to Benares, and is reported to have died here, or rather to have been translated hence.

His father is said to have been a Dakhní Brahman hailing from near Madras, by name Lakshman Bhatt. His mother's name was Illàmgárú. Tradition says that the parents were on their way to Benares, from Ayodhyá, when Ballabhácharya was born at a village in the District of Champáran, in the year 1535 Sambat, *i. e.*, 1478 A. D. He is stated to have become a disciple of Mádhavánand Tridandí at the age of five, and to have manifested great precocity, holding disputations with most learned pandits at a very early age, and coming out victorious. His father died while he was still a boy. He appears to have left Benares, and made long tours over different parts of India. These tours are modestly referred to as "Digbijai," *i. e.*, "Conquest of the world," and doubtless refers to his discussions with, and victories over, pandits.

Ballabhácharya is in the Vaishnavite succession, but his energies were devoted, not to the spread of the worship of Rám, but of the incarnation of Vishnu in Krishna and Rádhá. The sect which regards him as their founder, the Rádháballabhís, identifies itself with the worship of Krishna, especially of the boy Krishna and Rádhá, and represents a distinctly sensuous aspect of Hinduism. Asceticism and celibacy are not encouraged, and worship of their favourite deity is held not to be inconsistent with a very genuine appreciation of the good things of the material side of life. The temple in Benares which is most closely identified with this aspect of Hinduism is the temple of Gopál Mandir. It is most largely resorted to by the wealthy traders, merchants, and bankers of the city.

Ballabhácharya is said to have ended his days in Benares, at a house near the Ganges, by Hanumán Ghát. Tradition has it that he either fell into, or jumped into the river, from which he ascended to heaven in the form of a flame of fire. He is said to have passed away in 1530 A. D. at the age of 52.

Ballabhácharya was a voluminous writer in both Sanskrit and Hindi. Babu Harischandra mentions twenty-four works as having been written by him, including a commentary on the Bhágavat Purán, entitled "Subodhiní."

He left two sons and many disciples. There is a house near Hanumán Ghát still in possession of his followers.

TULSI DAS.

A little place hardly better than a shed, hidden away at the back of Gopál Mandir, and a ramshackle old house by the Ganges, are the only material memorials, in Benares, of the sweetest poet that she ever had, but Tulsí Dás has a better memorial then Benares can build him in the "Rámáyan," which stands alone in Hindi literature for its great merit and its widespread fame. Moreover it is not merely *fame*, the people know and love the book. The cultured recognise its beauty, and the very ignorant are capable of revelling in it. You may find a country yokel, sitting in his village at night, with a tattered copy of the book open before him, in the dim light afforded by a shred of cotton wick floating in a spoonful of oil in an open saucer, gracefully swaying his body to the metre of the poem, or *his* metre of it, droning away at the chaupáís and dohás of the Rámáyan with as much gusto, as that with which an English villager may pipe forth the verses of some old hymn rich in memories and experiences.

A Hindi writer has said :—

"Tulsí the sun, Súrdás the moon, Keshava Dás a constellation.
As for the poets of the present, they here and there sparkle about like fireflies."
And Tulsí Dás may well be called the " Sun " among the Hindi poets.

Of the life of Tulsí Dás not very much is known. His father's name is said to have been Atmárám, a Bráhman, and his mother Hulasí. The child's birth happened under such an unlucky star, that in accordance with current usage under such circumstances, he was abandoned by his parents.

His birthplace is uncertain. Hastinápúr, Hájípúr, and Rájpúr, all claim the honour. For a time he lived in Solon. It was at Ayodhyá, in the year 1575, that he commenced to write the Rámáyan, he finished it in Benares, where he came to reside. He wandered about much, but returned to Benares, and died here in the year 1623.

Tulsí Dás is said to have married early, his wife's name being Ratnáwalí, and to have had one son, Tárak, who died quite young. The poet was passionately fond of his wife. The story runs that on one occasion she had gone off for a visit to her parents' home. Tulsí Dás could not endure her absence, and followed her, she, (whether out a very pious mind, or annoyed, or out of sheer mischief, is not evident told him that he ought to be ashamed of himself to follow her about in such a way, and to be enamoured of her bodily charms, why did not he spend the power of his devotion and his life on Rám. The husband took her too seriously and resolved to follow her advice. She felt that things were going too far, but was unable to turn him from the resolve which he had formed at her suggestion. Rám found a devotee, she lost a husband. Once again in later life she met him, and then desired to share his simple life but her wish was not gratified.

Many incidents about his life are current, but most of them are doubtfully attested, and partake of the marvellous. Two are worth giving as they indicate the estimate of his character which gave rise to such stories. It is related that a thief once attempted to break into his house, but found it guarded by an armed man, a second attempt, on another night, was frustrated in the same way. Afterwards the poet heard from the thief's own lips about this watchman, and was greatly surprised, as he kept no such guardian servant. Then the truth dawned on him, it was his beloved and divine Rám who had thus assumed human form, that he might guard the treasures of his servant. Tulsí Dás was so ashamed of having caused his Divine Master such trouble, by attempting to hoard wealth, that he gave it all away, and decided that he would be true to the vow of poverty henceforth.

The second story is associated with the Emperor's Court at Delhi. The Emperor demanded that the poet should perform a miracle in his presence. He would not, and denied his ability to do so. The Emperor sought to flatter him into compliance by saying "You can do anything," to which the reply came, with more truth than courtliness, " You lie, recognise only Rám."

Tulsí Dás wrote many works. Some very long lists are given, but from these, twelve books only are generally accepted as genuine. The most popular of all is the Rámáyan, or as he himself called it "Rám Charit Mánas," *i. e.*, The sacred lake of Rám's doings. This is a poem of some 12,800 lines. It is the story of Rám told in most delightfully colloquial Hindi. Occasionally it is referred to as a translation of Válmíkí's Sanskrit Rámáyan, but this is quite a mistake, the story of Rám is given in both, but Tulsí Dás's is quite an original work.

Another poem, the Binaya Patriká, Dr. Grierson regards as superior in some respects to the Rámáyan even, but it is a far more difficult book, and not easy for even an Indian to understand, mainly owing to the expressions being so concise and elliptical. I rejoice to hear that a very able Hindi scholar is undertaking to bring out a Hindi paraphrase of the book, to help would-be readers.

Probably Tulsí Dás possessed no originality as a thinker, he was a devotee and a poet, and helped, as no other Hindu has, to lead the common people on to richer conceptions of the graciousness and lovableness of God. There is much that we cannot agree with, but his teaching made for truth and righteousness and purity. He, in common with others, who taught along the lines of the doctrine of Rámánuj and Rámánand, did much to counteract the evil influence of teachers like Ballabhácharya, who fostered the Krishna cult.

Benares may well be proud to have been the home of Tulsí Dás.

CHAPTER X.

THE PANCHKOSI ROAD.

THE Panchkosí Road encircles Benares, and within it all the ground is supposed to be peculiarly sacred. "Panch" or "pánch" means *five*, and "kos" is a measure equalling about two English miles, it is called the Panchkosí road because it roughly forms a semicircle from the Bishwanáth Temple at a radius of five kos. The word *semicircle* is used because the road could not *encircle* Benares at a five kos radius without crossing the Ganges, which it does not.

Whatever terms are used they will not work out exactly. Mathematically, the road ought to be about 25 miles from start to finish, as a matter of fact it is not much short of fifty.

A European visitor to Benares is not likely to attempt the pilgrimage, but no description of Káshí would be complete without some notice of this Panchkosí Road. Some parts of it, *e. g.*, those along the bank of the Ganges, are not traversable by a wheeled vehicle, and most parts would be very rough on the springs. This is, however, a matter of no importance, as one of the essentials for securing merit by the pilgrimage is to traverse the whole distance on foot, except in the case of extreme old age or sickness. Generally speaking, it is a delightfully soft road, not by reason of mossy turf, but on account of the great depth of dust.

One Hindu friend of mine tells me that he bicycles round the whole distance every Sunday, excepting during the rainy season, when he has to give it up as there is no regular boat service on the road. Whether by bicycling he is not evading the stipulations, is open to question, but considering the road, a journey like this in the hot season, or any other season, is an arduous task, and might be considered a work of merit.

The road is one of considerable beauty and picturesqueness. For most of the length it is finely shaded by trees, and there are many tanks and temples at various points on the road.

Apparently the virtue of the pilgrimage is of most special application to the residents of Benares. The fact is recognised that in spite of the intrinsic sanctity of Benares, it is just possible for a resident to commit sin, this has actually occurred more than once. But here a great difficulty arises, a sin committed in Benares is so heinous that it cannot be atoned for in the most sacred spot in Benares itself. A pilgrimage round the Panchkosí is the only way out of the difficulty. As a matter of fact, however, large numbers of others besides residents of Benares do the pilgrimage. This is understandable, for even those who have come as pilgrims to the City may have committed some trespass during their stay. How sins can be dealt with that are committed on the Panchkosí Road I do not know. Great care is demanded in the conduct of the pilgrims during the journ.y, and let it be fully recognized that there is much real devoutness on the part of many of those who follow these time-honoured practices. However worthy of blame they may be esteemed who trade on the ignorance of the people, in initiating and maintaining such useless rites and ceremonies, yet there is much, very much, to admire in the devotion with which some worshippers carry out the teachings of their preceptors in fulfilling tasks of great difficulty and hardship. And it may be that it would be wise to be gentle in making charges of superstition, superstition is not quite a thing of the past in Christian lands.

One of the very special times for this Panchkosí pilgrimage is when "malmás" occurs. This is an extra month which has to be intercalated about every third year to keep the Hindu calendar correct. Quite recently it fell in the very hottest season of the year, and yet thousands upon thousands faced the weary hot tramp of nearly fifty miles. They would probably greatly appreciate the injunction which requires them to bathe twice during the day.

The pilgrimage is no casual walk round, but must be undertaken in due form. Having bathed, the pilgrim must first do "puja" (worship) at Bishwanáth Temple, and Dhundráj, after this he must make his "sankalp," *i. e.*, formally express his resolve to perform the pilgrimage. He then proceeds to Manikarniká Kund, and from there proceeds southwards along the bank of the Ganges. On reaching Assí Ghát he should turn aside and visit the Durgá Temple (Monkey Temple), return to Assí Ghát, and then breaking away from the bank of the Ganges enter upon what may be more specifically called the Panchkosí Road.

The first stage ends at the village of Kanhawá. This is more generally known by the name of the celebrated temple there, Kardameshwar. This temple is the finest on the whole road. It is unusually well situated, with a large tank lying between it and the road. It bears distinct marks of age, but being most strongly built is in a good state of preservation. The pilgrim settles in here for the night, having travelled some six or seven miles from Manikarniká.

It should be mentioned that there are along the road numerous shrines and temples, which will be pointed out by the guide, if one has been engaged, and possibly in the case of the very devout something in the way of worship will be offered at every spot of note.

The second day's march is to Bhímchandí, a march of about eight miles. This is quite a small village. I well remember my first sight of it. It was just after the huge mela held in Allahabad, and large numbers of pilgrims from various parts of India had come to Benares, and were undertaking the Panchkosí pilgrimage. The little village was thronged with these strangers, in their various styles of dress, and varieties of colour, and presented a picture which an artist might well have been fascinated with.

The third day's journey is to Rámeshwar, a distance of ten miles. This has various objects of interest on the way. Almost at the start is a very fine tank and temple at Rájá ká Táláo, belonging to the Mahárájá of Benares. About three miles further along the road there is another very fine tank, with a part specially screened off, by stone screens, for the use of women. Other quaint and interesting spots are also passed. Rámeshwar itself is picturesquely situated on the bank of the river Barná, with a group of temples and a bathing ghát.

The fourth day's march is a long one of fifteen miles to Kapildhárá. The journey is sometimes broken for the night at Shivapur, but this is not in the orthodox programme. Shivapur is a busy village on the high road to Jaunpur, and has other interests besides those belonging to religious side of life. It is only a few miles from Benares, and is becoming a somewhat busy mart. There are a few temples here, a broken tank, and several rest-houses for pilgrims. The special temple is one to the Panch Pándava, the five hero brothers of "Mahábhárat" fame.

From Shivapur to Kapildhárá the road is of a mixed character. For a short distance it is a metalled road, but in other parts is very deep in dust. There is one striking group of temples and the Golden Tank (Sone ká Táláo), the stone in the centre of which, and some figures scattered about the place, are supposed to be very old.

Kapildhárá itself is not a very striking place.

The last day's journey is by way of Barná Sangam (the meeting of the Barná and the Ganges). Crossing the Barná, the pilgrim once more joins the Ganges, walks along the bank as far as Manikarniká, where he should bathe, offer worship at Bishwanáth, and then proceed to the temple of Sákhí Bináyak (the witness Ganesh), to have the record made in the heavenly books that he has performed the meritorious pilgrimage.

In the hot season this journey must be a very trying one, but in the spring it must be like a religious picnic, for those who take it leisurely, and can appreciate the picturesque and the beautiful.

CHAPTER XI.

SARNATH.

THERE is no place in or around Benares which equals in interest that of Sárnáth, and recent excavations and investigations promise to throw not a little light on the past of this important centre of Buddhism.

It lies about 4 miles N.-W. from the Cantonments, and has a good driving road leading to it.

The name Sárnáth appears to be a shortened form of Sáranganáth (lord of the deer), and tradition assigns a deer forest to this spot.

Apparently Sárnáth had religious associations before the time of Buddha, and was known as Ishipattana (the abode of God), and Rishipattana (the abode of rishis or saints) the former name may have been connected with the worship of Mahádeva, which appears to be associated with Benares from very early times.

Among the "Játaka," or "Birth Stories of Buddha," there is one which connects the place with the derivation of Sárnáth, as the Deer Forest, and endeavours to associate Buddha with it before his historical appearance. It is such a characteristic story that it must be given. Buddha is supposed often to have visited the earth

The Dhamek at Sarnath,

before he was born as Gautama. In one of these manifestations he came as Lord of the Deer, and wandered about with the herds in the vicinity of the present Sárnáth. The Rájá of Benares, a keen sportsman, often made sad havoc among them. The Lord of the Deer, pained at this wanton destruction, appealed to the King, and gained his consent to an arrangement by which one deer should be furnished for the King's table day by day. The King assented to this, foregoing the pleasure which the hunting gave him, while the deer on their side remained true to their stipulation. On one occasion the turn came to a hind, who though not unwilling to sacrifice her own life for the common good, was anxious to save the life of her unborn little one, and therefore begged some respite. The Buddha generously took the hind's place, and betook himself to the King. The King struck by the remarkably fine appearance of the deer, asked why *he* should give himself up, probably arguing in his own mind that this was a singular use to make of his kingship. Buddha explained the circumstances. The King greatly marvelled at his magnanimity, and said "I am a deer in a human body, you are a man in the body of a deer." Not only was Buddha's life spared, but the deer were released from their engagement, and left free to wander in the forest unmolested.

Information about the Sárnáth of over twelve centuries ago is furnished by two Chinese travellers, devout Buddhists, who visited Benares and Sárnáth, and left some account of their journeyings. The first, Fa-Hien, apparently came in the beginning of the fifth century A. D., and Hiuen Thsang about two centuries later. (Between 629 and 645 A. D. is a date accepted by some.)

Fa-Hien's account is but scant, and records tradition, rather than giving the reports of his own observation. There is reference to the place being the haunt of deer.

to the austerities of the Buddha, the son of King Petsing (Suddhodana), whose daily food was one hemp seed and one grain of rice. There is also mention of five devotees, one of whom became a disciple of Buddha. Fa-Hien also mentions the existence of two monasteries.

Hiuen Thsang's account is much fuller. He gives a general description of Benares, and a more detailed one of Sárnáth. After mentioning the size of Benares, nct apparently the city, but the kingdom, "with a circuit of 667 miles," he passes on to a description of Sárnáth. His reference to 30 Buddhist monasteries, and 3,000 devotees, evidently refers to the kingdom of Benares, as he speaks, later on, of 1,500 devotees at Sárnáth. Not a little of his account is devoted to traditions about the Great Master. Hiuen Thsang was evidently a man of great devoutness, and of extreme simplicity and credulity, and it is possible that in some cases where he appears to be giving exact particulars grounded on personal observation, he may be unduly influenced by the fervid descriptions given by others, and writes from a mind glowing with pious imagination.

At present there is difficulty in making the ruins recently unearthed correspond with the description of this Chinese traveller, but there remains much more to be excavated, which may clear some things up. There is another fact to be considered, *viz.*, that there have been successive piles of buildings, thus making it difficult to ascertain which would correspond to those described by Hiuen Thsang. The ruins may represent building operations extending over seventeen centuries. Buddha commenced his work at Sárnáth probably during the 6th century B. C. and it is surmised that the place was demolished at the close of the 12th century A. D. This latter does not complete the limit, for doubtless much building may have been undertaken since that time although not in connection with Buddhism. For instance, the small brick building which surmounts the mound known as "Chaukhandi" was built at the close of the 16th century by Akbar, to commemorate a visit paid to the spot by his father Humáyun, who "deigned to come and sit here one day, thereby increasing the splendour of the sun."

It may be convenient for the visitor to have a short list of the principal objects of interest, and their relative positions :—

1. The Dhamek Tower, or Great Stupa. To the west of this is a Jain temple. West of this again is the present Museum. The new Museum is being constructed to the S.-W. of the Dhamek.
2. The "Main Shrine." A square block of brick and stone-work, about 30 yards square. Lying to the N.-W. of the present Museum.
3. The Asoka pillar. Immediately to the west of No. 2.
4. The Jagat Singh Stupa. About 20 yards south of No. 3.
5. The Monastery. Situated at some distance to the N.-E. of the Main Shrine.
6. The Chaukhandi Mound. On the left of the road a short distance before reaching the main body of ruins.

Fitful attempts have been made from time to time for the last hundred years or so to investigate the site of Sárnáth, but it is during the last few years, since Mr. F. O. Oertel commenced operations in 1905, that the most important discoveries have been made.

The first excavations were made in no spirit of antiquarian research. In 1794, Babu Jagat Singh, the Díwán of the Mahárájá of Banares, was undertaking building work in a mohallá of the city, named after its builder, Jagat Ganj, and Sárnáth was used as a quarry. Jagat Singh had enormous quantities of materials carried away from the debris scattered about at Sárnáth. Mr. Sherring says that he bore off a whole sacred tower. The foundations of what is referred to as the Jagat Singh stupa were investigated some years later by Major Kittoe and Mr. Thomas. Inside the stupa was found a stone box, in which was a marble casket containing some valuables. Nothing of the casket is now known, but the marble box was, later on, removed from the site where it had been left, and is now in the Museum at Calcutta. Many years afterwards part of an image of Buddha was obtained from Jagat Ganj, which had probably been found in the same place.

No particulars of this stupa are forthcoming. Whatever may have been in the centre has long since been removed, there remain now ring after ring of brickwork, which suggests that successive stupas had been built on the same spot, each one larger than the previous one, so as to include its ruins.

These stupas were, it would seem, monuments or memorials, probably erected to mark the exact spots associated with special incidents in the life of Buddha. Many, however, were probably erected by devout worshippers as a general expression of their devotion to their great master. Hiuen Thsang records that one stupa was erected to mark the spot where Buddha began to turn the wheel of the law, another to mark the place where the earliest disciples had their faith born, another where Buddha in a previous birth as an elephant had taken out and presented his tusks to a hunter who sought them, and concludes by saying "there are several hundred Viháras and Stupas, we only notice two or three, for it would be difficult to describe them in detail."

In 1815 Colonel C. Mackenzie carried out some excavations. In 1835-36 General Cunningham threw himself with considerable enthusiasm into the work, discovering many statues, now to be seen in the Museum at Calcutta. Equal care was not taken with all the finds, some were left on the ground, and General Cunningham relates how some forty statues were carried off "and thrown into the Barná river, to check the cutting away of the bed between the arches."

It would seem also that in the erection of the other bridge over the Barná, the ruins at Sárnáth were used as a quarry, and that quantities of stone were brought from it to use in the foundations.

Major Kittoe was the next investigator. He, apparently, carried on excavations both at Sárnáth and at Bakariyá Kund. Major Kittoe was not only an antiquarian but an architect and builder. He was erecting Queen's College at the time, and, it is said, used large quantities of stone brought from the ruins. We might reasonably conclude, however, that the stones were looked through before being used, and many sculptured stones were gathered together by Major Kittoe in the grounds of Queen's College. Some of these have since been removed to the Museum at Lucknow, and some to Sárnáth. Unfortunately Major Kittoe died before publishing the outcome of his investigations.

Mr. E. Thomas, Dr. F. Hall and others made some attempt to carry on the investigations, but probably the necessary funds were not forthcoming to accomplish much.

A new era of discovery was inaugurated by Mr. F. O. Oertel in 1905, and since then Mr. J. H. Marshall has spent much time in directing the excavations, and has enjoyed the assistance of Dr. Sten Kenow and Mr. W. H. Nicholls in dealing with the various treasures found.

Something further in the way of description may now be given of a few of the principal objects of interest already referred to.

1. *The Dhamek Tower.*—This had not to be ais-covered. It was the outstanding object which had always invited attention, and suggested the possibility of the reward that might follow investigation of the adjacent ground.

Major-General Cunningham devoted much time and labour to the examination of this tower, and most interesting extracts from his reports are quoted by Mr. Sherring in his book in Benares. A shaft was sunk down the centre of the stupa right to the foundation, and various galleries were made to ascertain its inner structure.

It stands 110 feet above the ground, but beneath this there is a very strong foundation of brickwork 28 feet in depth. Of this 28 feet, only 10 are below the original ground level, the remaining 18 above. Successive demolitions of buildings and other causes have apparently raised the level of the ground 18 feet. It would appear that previous to the present stupa another building existed, and that upon the remains of that the present Dhamek was erected.

The Dhamek is 93 feet in diameter at its base, and gradually lessens as it rises.

The lower portion, to the height of 43 feet, is of stone. This with the exception of the upper five courses is of solid stone throughout, the blocks being clamped together by iron cramps. The 10 feet above this has stone facing, but is brickwork inside. Above this level the tower is constructed of cemented bricks. General Cunningham concludes that this upper portion was possibly plastered over, and not even faced with stone, as the stone of the lower portion of the tower terminates at the same height

Carving on the Dhameck.

all round the building, and had there been stone-facing above this level the probability is that some of the stones would have been found in place.

In sinking the shaft, a slab of stone was discovered in the centre of the tower, over two feet in length by one foot broad, bearing an inscription, which has been translated as follows :—

> "Of all things proceeding from cause, their causes hath the Tathágata (Buddha) explained. The great Sramana (Buddha) hath likewise explained the causes of the cessation of existence."

The stone portion of the tower exhibits some very bold carving. To quote from General Cunningham :— "The lower part of the monument has eight projecting faces, each twenty-one feet six inches in width, with intervals of fifteen feet between them. In each of the faces, at a height of twenty-four feet above the ground, there is a semi-circular headed niche, five and a half feet in width, and the same in height. In each of the niches there is a pedestal, one foot in height, and slightly hollowed on the top, to receive the base of a statue; but the statues themselves have long disappeared...... There can be little doubt, however, that all the eight statues represented Buddhá......Judging by the dimensions of the niches, the statues must have been of life-size."

Running round the tower, immediately below the level of these niches, is a band nine feet in width, of very fine carved ornamentation. The band is split up into three narrower bands, the centre and larger one being, generally speaking, some geometrical design, the upper and lower being of flowered scoll work. Only in one place, the border on one of the recesses at the south-west corner, are living creatures introduced, these are some ducks, a frog, and also a tiny human figure, seated on a lotus, and holding a lotus in each hand. This ornamentation round the building shews considerable variety. It is not complete, in parts it is sketched out with a chisel, and it may be concluded that the carving was partly, or wholly, done after the stones had been hoisted into position.

This ornamentation represents Indian art at a high level; the design is bold, and the execution exceedingly fine. It bears most favourable comparison with most of the work of more recent times.

The fact that the ornamentation of the lower part of the tower was never completed suggests the possibility that the upper part may also have been unfinished, and that we have no means of ascertaining in what way the brickwork was to have been faced.

2. *The Main Shrine.*—The remains of this so-called "Main Shrine" are considerably to the west of the Dhamek. The ruin is about eighteen feet in height, and about ninety feet by ninety in extent. It is thought, from the thickness of the walls, that they were intended to support a "massive and probably lofty superstructure." The building is composed partly of bricks and partly of stones, the latter being apparently taken from older buildings. It is conjectured that the building, as now found, belongs to about the 11th century of our era, but an inscription on one of the stones points to the 2nd century B. C. as the date of one of the older buildings from which the materials were obtained.

There is a central chamber, opening to the east, and round this three other chambers, entered from the outside. In the one to the south is a most interesting four-square stone railing, surrounding the base of a stupa. Each side is eight and a half feet long, and about four and three-quarters high. There are square uprights, and rounded crossbars. The remarkable fact about this

Lion Capital, recently discovered.

railing is, that it appears to have been cut out of one solid piece of stone, and although very plain, exhibits most finished workmanship, the chiselling being so true and the polishing so excellent. The work is regarded as belonging to the age of Asoka. In this chamber was found a standing figure of Buddha.

3. *The Asoka Pillar.*—Close to this shrine has been found the most interesting relic of all,—a broken column with its capital. From an inscription on the part of the pillar still standing, it is clear that this is an Asoka pillar. The inscription is an edict enjoining obedience to the "order," and a warning against scism.

Whether this column is the one referred to by the Chinese traveller, Hiuen Thsang, is a question not to be hastily decided. He says, "A stone column has been set up, some seventy feet high. The stone is smooth as jade, and shines like a mirror. Those who pray fervently discern n it a multitude of figures on all occasions, every one sees these images that answer to his virtues or his vices. It was at this spot that Jou-lai (the Tathágata), after having attained to perfect knowledge, began to turn the wheel of the Law." A difference in size has been urged against the identity of that column and this, but the argument is not decisive, for the original size of the pillar now discovered is somewhat conjectural, though supposed to have been about 50 feet; again, we ought not to pin down the Chinese traveller to mathematical exactness. A greater difficulty is its position with reference to other buildings which are supposed to be referred to. But in the confusion which successive demolitions of buildings have effected, it would be unwise to place too much reliance on this. Perhaps the strongest objection that can be urged is the fact that Hiuen Thsang, in his description, makes no reference to the magnificent capital. One can scarcely conceive that this could have escaped his notice, or failed to secure mention. Though here again it must be remembered that the traveller was not an artist but a devotee.

The portion of the pillar at present standing is between sixteen and seventeen feet high, the upper portion has been broken off, and portions of this, together with the capital, were found lying between the rest of the column and the "Shrine."

The capital consists of four lions' heads, one looking in each direction, below these is a band shewing four wheels, and four small animals, a lion, an elephant, a bull, and a horse. This capital is a magnificent piece of sculpture, bold in design, no unnecessary detail, and executed in a manner that would do credit to a sculptor of any age, or country. The polish both on the column and capital is so good, that, as has been remarked, "it resembles granite rather than sandstone." A most remarkable feature about the pillar and capital is the wonderful preservation of their surface. The column is broken, and the lions' heads are not perfect, but three out of the four are, in the main, intact, and are as sharp and clear as though they had but now come out of the workman's hands. It seems well nigh incredulous how carving of such an age can appear so clean and sharp.

4. *The Jagat Singh Stupa.*—This has already been referred to, and as it is not one of the most interesting items, it need not detain us.

5. *The Monastery.*—This is the name given to a large block of buildings, parts of which have been unearthed at some distance to the north-west of the Dhamek. The excavations have not been completed. There existed, apparently, an extensive central building with wings. The basement was of excellent brick masonry, with a superstructure of stone. It is thought that these were among the later buildings erected at Sárnáth.

Museum at Sarnath.

6. *Chaukhandi.*—This lies at a considerable distance south-west from the Dhamek. It has already been mentioned that Akbar erected a building at the top of the mound, to commemorate his father's visit to the spot. The lower part probably marks the site of a very fine stupa, though no light has yet been given on the question as to why this one building should have been so far from the rest. It may be that excavations would reveal that this Chaukhandi was not so disconnected from the rest of the buildings as it now appears to be.

7. *Contents of the Museum.*—No attempt can be made to deal with these. It is hoped that when the new Museum is completed, these varied "finds" may be arranged by an expert, and a full descriptive catalogue published. This should prove helpful in the reconstruction of history, and prove of great service to students of Art in India.

A large standing statue of Buddha, and a huge carved umbrella should be specially noticed. From inscriptions on both of these it appears that they were erected at Sárnáth in the reign of Kanishka, *i.e.*, in the 1st century of the Christian era. Another very interesting item is a carved stone with eight panels portraying incidents in the life of Buddha. A huge figure of one of the Hindu gods should be observed, apparently of Mahádeva, but not under his usual form. Another object which should not be passed over is a very long stone, evidently from over a doorway. It is comparatively late work, but the execution of many of the figures manifests very skilled workmanship.

The Museum is full of objects of great interest, and a separate visit ought to be paid to Sárnáth to study them. One afternoon at Sárnáth is quite inadequate to get anything like an estimate of its treasures.

THE END.

INDEX.

Figures printed in darker type indicate the principal sections on the subject.